YOU CAN RETIRE EARLY!

YOU CAN RETIRE EARLY!

Everything You Need to Achieve Financial Independence WHEN YOU WANT IT

DEACON HAYES
Founder of Well Kept Wallet

Adams Media
New York London Toronto Sydney New Delhi

Adams Media
An Imprint of Simon & Schuster, Inc.
57 Littlefield Street
Avon, Massachusetts 02322

First Adams Media trade paperback edition NOVEMBER 2017

ADAMS MEDIA and colophon are trademarks of Simon and Schuster.

For information about special discounts for bulk purchases, please contact Simon & Schuster Special Sales at 1-866-506-1949 or business@simonandschuster.com.

The Simon & Schuster Speakers Bureau can bring authors to your live event. For more information or to book an event contact the Simon & Schuster Speakers Bureau at 1-866-248-3049 or visit our website at www.simonspeakers.com.

Interior design by Stephanie Hannus

Manufactured in the United States of America

10 9 8 7 6 5 4 3 2 1

Library of Congress Cataloging-in-Publication Data
Hayes, Deacon, author.
You can retire early! / Deacon Hayes, founder of Well Kept Wallet.
Avon, Massachusetts: Adams Media, 2017.
Includes bibliographical references and index.
LCCN 2017021311 (print) | LCCN 2017035252 (ebook) | ISBN 9781440599880 (pb) | ISBN 9781440599897 (ebook)
LCSH: Retirement income--Planning. | Finance, Personal.
LCC HG179 (ebook) | LCC HG179 .H3494 2017 (print) | DDC 332.024/014--dc23
LC record available at https://lccn.loc.gov/2017021311

ISBN 978-1-4405-9988-0
ISBN 978-1-4405-9989-7 (ebook)

Dedication

I would like to dedicate this book to my wife Kim and my two children, Finn and Avery. They mean so much to me and are the reason I started my journey toward financial independence.

Contents

Acknowledgments

I would like to acknowledge the following people for their insights and support in writing this book. I would like to thank my assistant Laurie Blank, who has worked numerous hours to help make this book possible. I would also like to thank Danny Fortes for his insights on the direction of this book.

I have the privilege to know personally three published authors who have had a great influence on me. I want to thank Steve Economides for all of his wisdom on what making a good book really means. I would like to thank Barry Asmus for his encouragement and insights over several cups of coffee. Also, I want to share my gratitude to Jeff Rose who connected me with this opportunity to write this book.

I would not be where I am today without the support and wisdom of those around me.

Introduction

It is possible for nearly anyone to retire long before the age of sixty-five, and in this book I'll show you the steps you need to take to plan your own path to early retirement. Having the money to retire early means you won't have to wait until you're sixty-five or even older to start living your life the way you want to live it. When you have the money to retire at fifty, forty, or even thirty years of age, your outlook on life will be different. You'll be able to stop working on someone else's terms and finally live life the way you want to.

People who have succeeded at retiring early make their decisions about life based on what seems right to them rather than what everyone else is doing. They make choices that allow them freedom; this means they are conscious of every financial decision they make and its impact on their retirement plans.

Different people have different concepts about what it means to retire early. For some, early retirement means being able to retire at age sixty. For others, their early retirement dream means to be able to retire at age thirty-five.

According to the Social Security Administration, full retirement age (FRA) is anywhere between age sixty-five and sixty-seven, depending on the year you were born. This is the time when you can start collecting full Social Security benefits. If you choose to retire and start drawing on your Social Security benefits before your FRA, you'll be penalized with smaller benefit checks.

However, by following the guidelines in this book, you can retire as early as you want without needing Social Security benefits. As I discuss how to formulate your early retirement plan (ERP), I'm going to help you plan as if you are not going to receive Social Security retirement benefits. In this way any Social Security retirement benefits you receive later on will be an addition to your income instead of something you'll depend on.

Regardless of what your target early retirement age is, there are many benefits to having the financial means to be able to retire early. People who are able to retire early have the freedom to travel, to spend time with family, to devote themselves to hobbies, to start their own business, or even to go back to school.

When you've planned your finances in a way that gives you the freedom to be able to quit your job, you can spend your time doing things you want to do and stop being stuck in a job that gives you nothing more than a biweekly paycheck.

What does early retirement really look like? The answer varies from person to person, but most agree that they want to retire early to allow themselves more time to do the things they really want to do.

Believe it or not, making a plan for early retirement is much simpler than it sounds. All you need is enough income-producing assets to provide for your living expenses for the rest of your life. Now let's look at how to achieve that goal.

CHAPTER 1

Start with *Why*

Is it really that farfetched to retire at fifty or even forty? Over the years, I have met people who have retired even earlier than that. You might think that retiring early means you must have a large income, but in fact it's possible, as we'll see, to do this with many levels of earnings. The key is to have a plan.

HOW MUCH DO I NEED TO RETIRE?

How much money you need in your nest egg in order to retire depends on two issues:

- What do you want to do in retirement?
- What do you anticipate your basic costs to be in retirement?

However, creating the plan isn't the hardest part of reaching early retirement. The most challenging task throughout your journey to retire early will be sticking to that blueprint.

You might think that only big purchases can derail you from your plan for early retirement, but the fact is that even small, everyday purchases can lead you off track. You may purchase a used car rather than a new one in order to save money, but if you are eating out three times a week rather than cooking at home, you're negating all the savings you made by forgoing that new-car purchase. That is the reason you need a strong *why*. Why do you want to retire early? Your *why* will be what motivates you through the tough times. It will give you the strength to say "no" to distractions that may hinder your ability to stay on track.

Discover Your *Why*

Early retirement looks different to everyone, but there are some common themes when people start dreaming about leaving their jobs. These can form the start of your search for your *why*.

Travel is a big one. Many people hope to spend more time traveling when they retire. Think about your travel aspirations: you might see yourself having coffee in a Paris café or hula dancing at a luau in Hawaii. Or, you might imagine something a bit more adventurous, such as exploring Machu Picchu in Peru or hiking the Appalachian Trail.

Maybe you want to do more than just visit a foreign country; instead your dream might be to live in a foreign country. The cost of living can be a lot less than in the States, especially as regards important considerations such as healthcare. For instance, did you know that you can live comfortably in Thailand on less than $2,000 per month?

DON'T UNDERESTIMATE

When assessing your postretirement costs, it's important to remember that many people substantially underestimate their cost of living after retirement. A good general rule is to add 10 percent to each budget category; this will account for underestimation of costs as well as inflation.

CHAPTER 1: START WITH *WHY*

Destinations such as Belize, Panama, and Costa Rica are becoming popular retirement sites for people who want to minimize their cost of living so that they can retire early.

If you retire early, you can do the things you want without being limited to the two weeks of vacation that you get from your employer. When your income isn't based on a job, you can spend a month, or even several months, really getting to know these amazing places. You can plan long-term vacations or live in a foreign country and experience life there as a local rather than just hitting the tourist spots.

Another popular reason people want to retire early is so they can spend more time with family and friends. When you are working a nine-to-five job you often have little energy left at the end of the day to spend quality time with the people you love.

Imagine never having to miss another one of your children's baseball games or ballet performances. Imagine being able to attend every friend and family get-together. Every birthday party. Every wedding. Every holiday celebration. You won't just show up and muddle through; you'll actually participate in the event with energy and enthusiasm.

HOW MANY YEARS WILL YOU BE RETIRED?

One early retiree who blogs about the subject, known simply as Mr. Money Mustache, told MarketWatch, "Based on a long-lasting hobby of reading books on stock investing, I realized that you can generally count on your nest egg to deliver a 4 percent return over most of a lifetime, with a good chance of it never running out. In other words, you need about twenty-five times your annual spending to retire."

That number of twenty-five times your anticipated annual spending is probably a good place to begin your calculations.

It's wise to consider overestimating the number of years you'll need to have money to survive postretirement. Retirees often underestimate their life expectancy and run out of money. So plan carefully! The more cash you have to live on after you retire, the better off you'll be.

Some people retire to pursue a dream. You probably have a passion or two you would like to pursue as well, something that would give your life meaning beyond relaxation and fun. Think back to when you were a child. What hobbies did you love back then? Did you create artwork or music? Did you read and make up stories? Did you do woodworking or build model cars? Do you still have time for any of those hobbies? Probably not. The passion for these hobbies can form an important part of your *why*.

Often our childhood interests involve things we would still enjoy doing, but they get pushed aside by adult responsibilities. Retiring early and being financially independent means that you can go back to those hobbies or find new interests, such as volunteering for causes that are important to you. Undoubtedly there are dozens of interesting and meaningful ways you would spend your time if you didn't have to work all day.

How to Find Your *Why*

Now it's time to make your own *why* list, which will help you identify why early retirement is important to you. This is the list that will motivate you to stick with your plan. Some people prefer to write their *why* list on a sheet of paper; others want to make it more prominent by using poster board to create an inspiring display, plastered with reminders of all of their dreams. It doesn't really matter how or where you record your *why* list as long as the method you choose ensures you'll see it regularly.

Once you decide how you are going to record your *why* list, start thinking about examples of what you want retirement life to look like. Where would you go? What would you do?

Your *Why* List

If you were able to retire right now, how would you spend your time? You can think about these things as you make the list that will help motivate you to stay on track with the financial goals that will get you to early retirement.

Determining why you want to retire early will do two things for you. First, it will help you determine the kind of life you want to live in retirement so that you can make a more concrete financial plan. Second, it will motivate you to keep reaching toward those financial goals. These are the reasons that figuring out your *why* is key to achieving your Early Retirement Plan, also known as your ERP.

This short exercise will help you discover why early retirement is important to you. Ask yourself the following questions:

1. What are the top five things I enjoy doing in life (e.g., spending time with family, working on my hobbies, volunteering at different venues, etc.)?
2. How much time do I spend doing those things now?
3. How much time would I spend doing those things if I were retired with no financial worries?
4. What else would I do with my time if I weren't tied to my job and had enough money?

You might find that you have several *why*s on your list, and that's okay. If you have several *why*s, prioritize them in order of "most important" to "least important."

DO IT TOGETHER

If you have a spouse, it's important to do this exercise together. Your spouse's *why*s will be just as important as yours in an early retirement plan. Write out a description of a typical day for you in retirement. Have your spouse do the same thing. Then, compare them and write out a joint description of a typical retirement day.

A Retirement Lifestyle

After you've figured out why you want to retire early, you must determine what kind of lifestyle you'd need to be able to do the things you want to do. Could you simply cut back on your hours and work part-time in order to live the type of lifestyle you want? Or could you use your passion as a way to generate income? Could you do what you love to do in an area where the cost of living is cheaper, maybe in another area of the country or in another country altogether?

It's important to remember that retiring early isn't just about moving away from something (i.e., your job) but also about moving *toward* something else. Maybe you've always wanted to own your own business but didn't have the time or financial resources. What business would you own if you could choose any business in the world? Would you flip houses? Be a fishing guide at a resort? A tour guide in Italy?

Maybe you have always wanted to start a charity. What type of charitable organization would you found? Would you help feed those who don't have enough to eat? Provide assistance and resources to the homeless? Help build homes, schools, and clean water wells in third-world countries?

ROGER BANNISTER AND THE IMPOSSIBLE MILE

Have you ever heard of Roger Bannister? He is the first guy to ever run a mile in four minutes. People told him that it was humanly impossible to do it, yet he did. You know what happened after he showed the world it was possible? Hundreds of people ran a mile in under four minutes. He was an inspiration to others by his example, and you can be as well.

Early Retirement on Different Incomes

Early retirement doesn't depend on having a large income. It's possible to do it on a variety of incomes, provided you make a plan that works for you. Let's go over two case studies to see how it can be done. (The case studies in this book are for illustrative purposes, and may not be applicable to your lifestyle or geographic area.)

Case Study: Josh and Stephanie Plan Early Retirement

Josh and Stephanie are a couple in their early thirties. They've decided not to have kids. Josh is a plumber and Stephanie is a schoolteacher, but they're not living their dream life. In an ideal world, Josh and Stephanie would be living in Haiti, caring for the poor. Stephanie wants to teach children in Haiti, where there is no public education system, and Josh wants to show them how to build solid homes. Josh and Stephanie know that in order to start living their dream life, they're going to have to build up an investment account that will allow for enough income to cover the expenses they've calculated they'll need. Their gross annual pay is $125,000 a year. They've decided they need $4,000 a month in income to live comfortably in retirement. Although the cost of living in Haiti is very low, Josh and Stephanie want to have a plush financial cushion that allows them to give and live as they choose without too much worry about budgeting. What would it take to get there?

If Josh and Stephanie put $3,000 a month into an investment account and earn an average return on investment (ROI) of 8 percent, they'll have $1,012,819 (before taxes) in their investment account after fifteen years. Now, this is a financial model* based on certain fixed assumptions:

- They invest exactly $3,000 every month for fifteen years, no exceptions.
- They never take money out of the account.
- They put all the money they have allocated for investing into the stock market; investing in the stock market usually brings higher returns.
- Their investments yield an average of 8 percent ROI every year, and those earnings are left in the account.
- They pay taxes on the earnings out of their other income.

(*_Note_: Models in this book have been run using various online calculators, which may have a small effect on their results and comparability.)

Speaking of taxes, it may be wise to invest some of this money in a Roth IRA (individual retirement account) to minimize taxes on the investment profits (more on Roth IRAs in Chapter 2).

Of course, this doesn't take into account financial setbacks (or windfalls) that happen in real life. But it does provide a good model of what you can achieve when you stick to a consistent savings plan.

If Stephanie and Josh continue to invest at a postretirement earnings rate of 4 percent (postretirement monies should be in lower-risk investments), they will be able to withdraw $4,000 a month for living expenses over the next fifty years.

This is a basic model that covers Stephanie and Josh's estimated expenses after retirement; however, there are also other factors they will need to consider as they determine how much money to put away each month. First, their rate of return may decrease if they reallocate their investments over time. Most financial experts suggest that as recipients get older they move investment accounts from a 70/30 stock/bond allocation toward one that is heavier on bonds and lighter on stocks (more on this later). I've accounted for some of that decrease in the model by using an 8 percent rate of return (the stock market average is roughly 11 percent at this time). However, it wouldn't hurt if Josh and Stephanie moved their target income up to $5,000 per month and started early retirement with a larger balance to account for potential fluctuations in their ROI.

Also, adding a decent-sized buffer to their investment account will help cover any potential increases in their cost of living due to inflation or underestimation of expenses, as well as any income taxes they have to pay.

But, you may be saying to yourself, those sorts of numbers don't apply to me, because unlike Stephanie and Josh I have children or plan on having them, which means my expenses will be higher than Josh and Stephanie's. A lot of people who want to retire early have kids. The challenge of having children—and thus ongoing expenses, including college tuition—leads many people to think that retiring early just isn't possible for them.

It's also true that many people who'd like to retire early have substantially lower incomes than that of Josh and Stephanie. This makes them think that they're doomed to continue working until they reach their full retirement age.

In fact, it's possible to take early retirement both with kids and with a lower income—it just takes some careful planning. As well, it's probable that you won't be able to have the range of choices in retirement that Josh and Stephanie have. Given Josh and Stephanie have decided to live their postretirement lives in a low-cost-of-living country they will need much less money to survive on than they are saving for, so that they can have an abundant surplus of cash each month to spend as they wish. Your early retirement plan funds may not give you such high liquidity, but you can still save enough to retire early.

Case Study: Ethan and Jessica Plan Early Retirement on a Lower Income

Ethan and Jessica are a two-income couple in their early thirties with three kids. Their son is twelve years old, and their two daughters are ten and eight. Ethan is an IT technician and Jessica works part-time in a dental office. Their total family income is roughly $72,000 after taxes—lower than our previous case study—and they make the most of every dollar with stringent savings and frugal financial decisions, including not taking on debt other than the mortgage on their modest home. Their $90,000 mortgage has a $725 monthly payment, which includes their property taxes and insurance.

Jessica and Ethan plan to retire early. Their plan includes paying off their mortgage before retirement, which is essential given their modest income. With their home paid off, the couple figures they'll need about $2,200 a month to live on after they retire. Although this may seem like a small amount of money, it is not uncommon for couples who have no debt and who live in areas of the country with a lower cost of living to get by on a monthly income in this range.

WHAT IS A 529 PLAN?

A 529 plan is a college savings plan legally known as a "qualified tuition plan." A 529 plan is opened by a student, parent, or other account holder and designates a beneficiary for whom the funds will be used to pay for college expenses. Not all 529 contributions are tax deductible, but the earnings grow and can be used tax free as long as they are used for qualified college expenses. See more on 529s here: www.sec.gov/reportspubs/investor-publications/investorpubsintro529htm.html.

Ethan and Jessica also know that by the time they retire in twenty years, their kids will be grown (the youngest will be twenty-eight), moved out (the possibility of adult children moving back home is addressed in Chapter 10), and finished with college, so the couple will have fewer expenses.

PAYING FOR COLLEGE AND WEDDINGS

It's important to remember when making your early retirement plan—especially on a lower income—that sometimes parents don't pay for their children's college costs or wedding costs. Many find these costs are a financial impossibility and make sure their children understand that costs obtained in adulthood will be the children's responsibility.

With their $6,000 combined monthly take-home pay, Ethan and Jessica have carefully budgeted money toward saving for their kids' futures, building an emergency fund, and paying the mortgage. Those fixed monthly expenditures include:

- $725 mortgage payment
- $200 deposit into an emergency fund
- $300 toward 529 plans ($100 toward each child's college education)
- $300 toward weddings or home purchases ($100 for each child)

That leaves them $4,475 to cover all of their other monthly budget items. Since Ethan and Jessica take a modest approach to spending, they are able to stretch that money to cover their basic household needs and put money toward their early retirement plan. They figure that they can comfortably put $1,150 per month toward their early retirement plan.

If Ethan and Jessica consistently invest that $1,150 every month for twenty years, and achieve an 8 percent annual rate of return (the same assumption we made in the previous case study), they'll end up with an investment account balance of $682,036 before taxes. (Remember, the model assumes they never skip a month, put away a different amount, or take out money.)

At a postretirement 4 percent investment rate (remember, the post-retirement investment monies should go into lower-risk investment options), this will give the couple $2,273 per month to live on. This is a little higher than Ethan and Jessica's postretirement income goal of $2,200 a month.

Planning for a buffer, which can help cushion against inflation and cost-of-living increases, is never a bad idea. If Ethan and Jessica could find a way to add another $100 a month to their early retirement investment account, they could accumulate nearly $60,000 more by the time they retire (as long as we stick to the same set of assumptions), which is a reasonable buffer for cost-of-living increases and inflation.

As mentioned earlier, we're not taking Social Security checks into account as we figure these numbers. That way whatever Social Security benefits Ethan and Jessica receive will be bonus income when they reach their full retirement age.

It's easy to see from the previous scenarios that early retirement is possible under vastly different income situations. You just need a do-able plan to get you there.

Once you have your early retirement plan (ERP) in order and are doing what needs to be done to achieve that dream, it is likely that you will start to inspire those around you to make better financial choices as well. Your loved ones will see that you are actually achieving your goals and not just talking about achieving them. They'll see that your plan and the steps you are taking to work that plan are producing solid results.

Keep Your Plan Visible

Once you have a clear vision of the reasons why early retirement is important to you and what your life in retirement will consist of, it is important to keep this picture at the forefront of your mind at all times. I already mentioned the possibility of creating an inspirational poster. As well, daily reminders such as a picture on your fridge or a sticky note on your mirror are helpful. You can set the desktop on your computer to a picture that represents your vision or even change your password to a word that reminds you of your goal.

You need to do whatever it takes to keep the idea of early retirement front and center. If you don't, life will get in the way and your dreams will once again be moved to the back burner. It might seem unnecessary to take these steps when early retirement seems so far off, but it is because it is so far away that these steps are needed. Keeping your *why* in the foreground will motivate you to make the daily choices that will bring you closer to your early retirement goal. Life will present daily opportunities to get off track. You will need these daily reminders to help you remember what is truly important.

When Is the Right Time to Retire?

The "right" time to retire should be when you decide it is. It will largely depend on what kind of retirement you decide you want. You need to have the financial steps in place to back up your plan. Don't let the crowd determine when you should retire; make a retirement plan that is best for you.

A Personalized Plan

In the next chapter I'll talk about how to develop a personalized plan that fits your specific early retirement goals, dreams, and time frame. I'll share different paths to achieving financial independence so that you can determine which type of investments best fit your personality and your comfort level. There are many roads to early retirement, so it's wise to figure out a road for getting there that fits who you are and what you want to accomplish, as well as the lifestyle you want to live when you retire.

CHAPTER 2

How to Develop a Personalized Plan

Your personalized plan is the roadmap you create that will get you on the path to early retirement. Your plan may have ideas and pieces that you gather from others, but the plan itself has to be your own. It has to fit you and your individual goals and interests, and be developed in a way that works with your personality type. If you're married, your plan has to be agreeable to your spouse as well. In this chapter you'll want to start taking note of different ideas and information that will help you draw up your own plan for growing the wealth necessary to retire early.

Some of the steps here might seem simple, but they're all necessary to create the type of plan that will help you cover all your bases as you build the foundation of your retirement nest egg.

What Is the Lifestyle You Want in Retirement?

The first question you should ask yourself is, "How do I/we want to live in retirement?"

- Is the lifestyle you want in retirement similar to how you live now?
- If you currently have $4,000 in monthly expenses, do you expect to have that amount in retirement?
- Do you want to live better and have more money in retirement?
- Would you be okay with living on less money than you have now?
- Do you want to drive new cars, travel internationally, and spend as you please during retirement, or are you content to live a modest lifestyle with budgeted spending, paid-for inexpensive cars, and minimal domestic travel?

These are some of the questions you need to ask yourself as you calculate your postretirement financial needs.

As you're determining these needs, refer to the list you made as directed in Chapter 1 that details the *why*s behind your reasons for wanting to retire early. Depending on what those *why*s are, your postretirement spending could be very different from the way you spend your money today.

For instance, if your plan after early retirement is to go back to school and get a degree, you'll need to account for tuition and other school costs in your monthly expenses. If your plan is to move to a different part of the country or the world, you'll need to research the costs of living in that area and determine how this will affect your budget. It will take some work to account for every potential cost associated with the different *why*s on your chart as you plan your expected postretirement financial needs. Let's talk a bit about potential postretirement expenses and how you can determine a target savings rate for them as you make your ERP.

Going Back to College

If you plan to attend college after retirement, you'll want to determine how much it will cost based on the school you want to attend and the type of degree you want to earn. Since most early retirement plans take at least ten years to fund, you'll need to adjust for future expenses: add in at least a 20 percent buffer for increased tuition costs since you likely won't be going to school for at least a decade. College costs have risen by between 9 and 13 percent in the past five years, so a 20 percent increase is an acceptable estimate for a ten-year wait.

Let's say you want to earn your postretirement degree in social work after you retire early and the current cost for a year's tuition at the in-state college in your state is $20,000, not including room and board. As you determine your postretirement financial needs, you'll want to include the $80,000 for four years of college tuition, plus a 20 percent buffer of $16,000 for rising tuition costs.

In other words, you'll plan for at least $96,000 of your postretirement income to be targeted for college attendance. Sites such as BigFuture.org can help you determine the current tuition and other costs of the schools you're considering attending.

Moving to a Different Area

In the same way, if you plan to live in a different state or country after you retire, you will need to research what the cost of living is in that area. Websites such as Bankrate.com and Numbeo.com have calculators that can help you compare the cost of living in your current location with that in other cities or countries.

When determining cost-of-living changes for moving to a different area, it's important to take into consideration all costs, including rental or home purchase, food, utilities, local taxes, transportation, clothing, entertainment, and more. The reason for doing a comprehensive study such as this is that whereas some areas might have lower costs for housing, they may have higher tax rates or higher costs for gasoline or public transportation. In order to get the full picture of what your postretirement costs will be in another area, you need to take all significant costs into consideration and calculate your postretirement income needs accordingly.

HEALTHCARE

An important cost in your retirement is healthcare, one that will increase as you get older. In this respect, there are a lot of advantages to living outside the United States. Many countries offer free or very cheap quality healthcare. This is an important issue to research if you're thinking of retiring abroad.

No matter where you may consider living, packing up all of your belongings and moving to another location comes with expenses, especially if you are moving far away from your current location. A better option might be to keep a low-cost home base in your current city, one that allows you the freedom—financial and otherwise—to do what you want without giving up your current location. Studio apartments, condominiums, and townhomes are all potentially inexpensive options for a home base that require little maintenance and have a minor impact on your net worth.

Some retired couples also choose to live in an in-law apartment at the home of an adult child or other relative. If your goal in retirement is to be able to travel a lot, it may be cost-effective to keep an inexpensive home base that's available when you are not traveling. Many early retirees find this is a better alternative to moving to a cheaper state or country.

Charitable Work

If your plan is to spend your time doing charitable work, you'll need to account for any travel costs associated with where you want to do your charity. As well, there may be other expenses associated with it. For instance:

- Will you be doing your work in your home city or traveling to other parts of the world?
- Will you keep a home base such as a home or apartment?
- Who will care for your home while you are away?
- Where will you stay if you are doing charity work away from home?
- How will you provide for food, transportation, and other living expenses if you are doing charitable work away from home?
- Are you planning on contributing cash as well as your time in your ventures? If so, have you accounted for cash donations to charity in your early retirement plan?

Take some time to do a thorough assessment of all basic and extra costs you may incur when you're retired. Make sure you're including all living expenses including housing, transportation, and healthcare, as well as any money that might be needed for extras such as gifts. Make a rough budget that can give you a clear idea of how much money you'll need each month after you retire. Be on the liberal side with your expenses and try not to underestimate them, especially medical expenses.

Healthcare Costs Add Up

Our health tends to deteriorate as we age. Look at your family history to help determine what types of health problems you may experience as you get older. While taking good care of yourself by eating well and staying active can help reduce potential medical expenses, it's still a smart idea to give your plan a substantial cushion for medical costs as you determine your postretirement budget.

The latest studies show that a couple retiring in 2016 at age sixty-five will need more than $260,000 for healthcare premiums over the course of their retirement—and that doesn't even include dental, vision, co-pays, and out-of-pocket costs. Those other costs can also run higher than $200,000, so it's important to plan for them as well (especially if any health issues, such as diabetes or heart disease, run in your family). AARP.org has a healthcare costs calculator that can help you determine what your additional healthcare expenses may be postretirement.

If you have additional insurance coverage that will help cover health-care costs, that's great. However, as you budget for postretirement expenses, you need to be sure to include the annual premium costs for those insurance policies. Another way to keep health costs low after early retirement is to consider joining a healthcare-sharing ministry, which can take the place of insurance. The monthly premiums are generally much lower than what traditional insurance companies charge and many healthcare-sharing ministries offer coverage up to $1 million.

MEDICARE

Although the government insurance program Medicare currently covers a lot of medical costs for those over age sixty-five who enroll in it, it doesn't cover everything. For instance, to date if you experience long-term hospitalization, after 150 days you'll be responsible for the entire cost of the stay. It also doesn't cover expenses for things like basic dental care or glasses. On the other hand, it will cover things such as doctor's visits, trips to the ER, and health counseling for lifestyle changes (for instance, if you're trying to quit smoking). These coverage parameters are based on the Medicare rules at the time of publication. Know that if Medicare rules change, you may not be able to expect the level of coverage currently provided by Medicare. Therefore it's important to plan for a buffer in your estimated healthcare savings in anticipation of potentially changing Medicare coverage amounts.

In addition, consider getting long-term care insurance coverage in case you become disabled or sick to the point that you need chronic medical care. According to the American Association for Long-Term Care Insurance, more than 88 percent of new claims happen after age seventy. Financial expert Dave Ramsey says you can consider waiting until you are sixty to get this type of insurance, but that may lead to higher annual premiums.

COSTS INCH UP WITH INFLATION

When determining how much cash you need to fund your ERP, don't forget to account for inflation. Your cost of living will increase, and it's important to add a cost-of-living adjustment (COLA) to your expected monthly expenses to cover that.

On average, inflation currently runs at about 3 percent per year. You can calculate the inflation factor on your own in a spreadsheet program, or use a free online resource.

Other Expenses

Other than insurance, you should account for bigger items such as travel, vehicle purchases, and other major expenses monthly by estimating your annual expenditures in these areas and dividing by twelve. Don't forget to consider how many years you want to be able to live on your retirement income. The earlier you retire, the more years you'll need to have income. To give you an idea of how one early retiree budgets for his expense, see Mr. Money Mustache's budget: www .mrmoneymustache.com/2016/04/01/mmm-spending-2015/.

Websites such as Bankrate.com have retirement income calculators that can help you determine how much cash you'll need to retire, taking into account your estimated monthly expenses and inflation. This calculator also allows for whether or not the investment is tax-deferred. Many retirement accounts (such as 401(k)s and traditional IRAs) are tax-deferred, meaning you don't pay taxes on the money you put in, but you will have to pay taxes on both your contributions and earnings as you take out money. Roth IRAs don't offer an immediate tax break (they're funded with after-tax money), but as long as you follow the withdrawal rules, you won't pay taxes on any of the earnings. Regular investment accounts don't offer the same tax benefits; all the money you put in is after-tax investment money, and you pay tax every year on the earnings. These distinctions are important because the amount you'll have to pay in taxes after you retire will vary based on what types of accounts hold your investments. You'll want to be sure your ERP investment funds include money to cover any taxes payable on your investment earnings.

This Bankrate.com tool is great for helping you figure out your ERP target dollar amount, the amount you'll need to have saved before you retire, and how much additional money you'll need to save each month to make up for any projected goal shortfalls.

Once you've determined a realistic amount for your expected monthly expenses postretirement, you can then move on to the next step: modifying your existing finances so that you can put money toward your goal of retiring early.

Start with a Budget

A successful early retirement plan (ERP) starts with developing a budget to manage your current income and expenses. People often shy away from the idea of living on a budget because at first glance it can seem restrictive, and they don't like the idea of putting limits on their spending. But the truth is that a budget really provides you with freedom. It helps you eliminate wasteful spending that is taking you away from your financial goals and helps you make a plan to get to financial freedom faster.

How many times have you asked yourself, "Where does my money go every month?" Does it ever seem like you should have money left over at the end of the month but you never do? When you know where your money is going, you can make a concrete plan for reaching early retirement. If you don't have a handle on your budget, you can end up wasting hundreds of dollars every month on small purchases.

Building a Budget

Making a budget is really pretty simple. Start by writing in the income column the total net cash (meaning all the money you actually receive, after reductions such as taxes) you have coming in each month from each source. Sources may include your paycheck, any money you have coming in from a business or rental property you own, and interest and dividends earned on savings and investments.

In the expense column you'll write down all of your monthly expenses. Don't forget to set an average monthly budget amount for things you don't buy every month such as clothing, car repairs, insurance, or gifts. If you haven't budgeted before and are unsure about what you spend each month or year in a given budget area, look back at the past twelve months' worth of credit card statements or checking account statements. This can help you discover any additional annual expenses you may have forgotten about.

Here's a simple example:

Monthly Income	
Take-home pay #1	$4,500
Take-home pay #2	$3,500
Total take-home income	$8,000
Monthly Expenses	
Rent	$1,500
Utilities	$500
Transportation	$700
Groceries	$1,000
Entertainment	$500
Savings account	$800

To help determine how much you spend on gifts, make a list of who you buy for each year for birthdays or other holidays and set a target spending amount for each gift. I also suggest putting a finite amount into your budget for discretionary spending (meaning "unbudgeted" money that you can spend however you want) as well, both for you and for your partner. Having some play money each month will help make the budget less restrictive. It will also eliminate a lot of the arguments that happen over money since each of you has the ability to buy what you want (within reason).

Remember to include a monthly expense line for your emergency fund savings as well. As we've talked about (and will continue to talk about throughout the book), an emergency fund is a vital tool for covering any type of unexpected expense, such as home repairs, medical expenses, or car repairs.

Create Your Budget!

Stop reading now and create your budget. Visit the following website to help you get started: http://wellkeptwallet.com/resources. Don't worry about your budget being perfect; the goal for now is to know how much money you have coming in each month and what you are currently spending it on.

The linked form is in an Excel format and calculates all the figures as you fill it out. If you're not interested in using a form like this one but would rather have a cloud-based program, there are options available for budgeting such as Mint and Personal Capital. Chapter 9 discusses these programs in detail.

What Do Your Numbers Look Like?

Now that you have created your budget, what do the numbers show? Hopefully, your income is higher than your expenses, and there is money left over at the end of the month. This is your surplus. It's important for you to make sure that you have a surplus at the end of each month.

You might find out after creating your budget that you have a deficit at the end of the month—that is, you have more expenses each month than income. It's very common for people to spend more than they make; that's how they accumulate credit card and other types of debt. If you are sitting at a negative net number in your budget, you need to figure out a way to reduce expenses or increase income so you're left with a monthly surplus.

If you've gone over your budget thoroughly and find that reducing expenses isn't an option, you may need to approach the problem from the other side and increase your income. In fact, a lot of people find it easier to bring more money into the household than to figure out how to cut expenses. We'll talk about making more money in Chapter 3; for now let's focus on how to reduce expenses and how you can figure out which expenses can go.

Needs and Wants

One reason that many people have a negative number at the end of each month is because they spend too much money on "wants." This leaves them in the hole each month.

WHEN A NEED MEETS A WANT

It's easy for people to get confused too about the types of needs they should have. For instance, you do need transportation to work, but that transportation doesn't have to be a new $30,000 car. You do need clothes, but those clothes don't have to come with designer names on the tags.

A need is something you have to spend money on each month in order to live. Your list of needs is pretty short. It includes things like:

- Food
- Clothing
- Shelter
- Transportation
- Medical care

Pretty much everything else can be counted as a want. Cable television is a want. Eating out is a want. It's important to get the want/need definitions straight in your head as you make your plan. The faster you can eliminate those wants in your budget that aren't important to you, the faster you'll be able to start growing the kind of wealth that will allow you to retire early.

After you create your initial budget, it's a good idea to work each month on refining it. As you do this, think about what you're spending on needs and what you're spending on wants. Start to look for ways to cut down spending in both areas. In your budget, mark an N for a need and a W for a want. Make separate columns for your Ns and your Ws so that you can have a clear visual as you work on redefining your expenses and what they mean to you. Here's an example.

Need (N)		Want (W)	
Electric bill	$120	Eating out	$200
Gas for car	$300	Cable TV	$120
Clothing	$100	Gym membership	$85
Car insurance	$75	Entertainment	$150

When you break down your list of monthly expenses into Ns and Ws, you'll have a more concrete picture of what in your expense list is negotiable and what is not. This will help you to be more open-minded as you start on the next step of your plan: analyzing your expenses.

Analyzing Your Expenses

The piece of your budget that's going to make the biggest impact on whether or not you can retire early is the amount of money you have left over at the end of the month. The larger your surplus, the more money you'll have to put toward early retirement.

This is why getting a good handle on the difference between needs and wants is so important. As you study your budget, it's smart to analyze each line item expense. If you're married, do this with your spouse. If you're single, it's a good idea to have an accountability partner or mentor who can help you go over your budget. It's hard sometimes as an individual to have self-control. Look for someone who will be honest with you about your spending so you can take a candid look at your budget plans. Also, make sure that person is good with money and not a spendaholic.

Go over every expense in your budget. Ask yourself (and/or your spouse): are there expenses that I am willing to sacrifice for the opportunity to retire early? Ask this question about the big expenses as well as the smaller ones. They add up.

Evaluating Wants and Needs

Start by going through your wants. It's easiest to start there because these expenses are things that you don't need in order to survive. You can eliminate every one of them and still live a satisfying life. Challenge yourself as you go through your budget line items. See how little you can spend in each area in a given month, or try to eliminate the expense altogether. For instance, can you cancel your gym membership and start working out at home? Can you make a commitment to not eat out or to only eat out once a month?

After you've gone through your Ws list, it's time to take a closer look at your Ns list. Going through this list can be a bit more complex, but there's usually still room for improvement. For instance, you can shop around for cheaper car insurance rates and see if you can lower your insurance bill. You can shop around for Internet and phone service to see if you can get a better rate or switch to a less expensive plan. You can work to lower your energy bill by keeping the lights off and turning down the heat or using the air conditioner less. Look at each N expense and ask yourself how you can reduce it.

One of the biggest N expenses people have is housing. Something you'll want to consider as you think about your housing budget is "right-sizing." This means making sure you have the right-sized house for your needs so that you can save as much cash as possible and grow your net worth to a level where you can retire early. A different way to right-size your house may be to move to an area of the country where the cost of living is lower. Before you choose to move, however, consider the cost of moving (both financial and emotional), the need to find a new job and its rate of pay relative to the cost of housing, and, if you have children, the availability of decent schools in the areas where you are considering moving.

MAKING THE MOST OF YOUR SPACE

Did you know that families in Hong Kong often live in 400-square-foot apartments and that multiple generations live in that space?

I'm not saying you've got to cram ten people into a 400-square-foot apartment, but the story offers perspective on what you can live with in order to achieve your goals.

If you can't afford to move or don't want to, there are other ways you can reduce your housing costs. For instance, it may be possible to refinance your mortgage and get a lower interest rate. If you have a spare bedroom in your home, you can rent it out to a college student. Or you can rent storage space in your garage or basement. If you are paying private mortgage insurance (PMI), you may be able to get your PMI dropped when you have enough equity in your house (usually 20 percent).

LIVING SMALL

Here are some facts about tiny houses you might find interesting:
- The average tiny house is 186 square feet while the average traditional house in America is nearly 2,100 square feet.
- The average cost to build a tiny house is $23,000 if built by the homeowner.
- Sixty-eight percent of tiny house owners have no mortgage, compared to 29.3 percent of owners of standard-sized US homes.
- Approximately two out of five tiny house owners are over fifty years of age.

The housing issue is a tough one. Owning a mansion is one of the pillars of success in contemporary American society. But would that type of home keep you from retiring early? For instance, do you need to be paying for a 3,000-square-foot house when it's just you and your spouse and there are no plans to have kids?

Tiny Houses

One of the newest trends in housing is the tiny house movement. This movement advocates living in much smaller homes, usually with only a few hundred square feet of space.

One advantage they offer is that they're much cheaper to build than normal-sized homes—often between $20,000 and $50,000.

The tiny house movement is gaining in popularity as people start to question what it is they really want out of life. They ask whether the nine-to-five job is really an answer to their goals of living a fulfilled life. They wonder if having a large house is worth the time and money they sacrifice to live in it. A move to a tiny house may not be for you, but it's an alternative worth considering.

Each monthly expense you can reduce or eliminate, whether it's a want or a need, will mean more money toward being able to reach the financial freedom you need to become wealthy enough to retire early.

This doesn't mean you have to live in a camper for the next five years until you reach your goal, but budgeting does provide an opportunity for you to decide what's really important to you. It gives you a chance to sit down and take a good look at what your dreams are. Once you know what you really want out of life, it'll be easier to prioritize your spending on things that really matter to you.

Try the Cash Method

Variable expenses are those that fluctuate every month such as groceries, entertainment, eating out, vacations, gasoline, etc. They can all take out huge chunks of your expendable cash if you're not paying attention.

Using a cash-only system (commonly called a cash envelope system) for variable expenses can help you make sure you're not spending more than you want to in these areas. For those not familiar with this system, here's how it works. For every variable expense you have—such as the ones we talked about previously—take a small envelope and write the name of the expense on it (e.g., groceries, entertainment, clothing, car repair, etc.). At the beginning of each month, you put money in each envelope that correlates to the amount you've determined in your budget to spend in that area. For instance, if you've decided to spend $300 a month on groceries, put $300 in your grocery envelope at the beginning of each month. As you spend in a specific area, take cash out of the correlating envelope. When the money designated for that area is gone and the envelope is empty, you are finished spending in that budget area for the month. If for some reason you need to spend more money than you budgeted, you'll have to "steal" cash from another envelope, reducing your spending in that area for the month.

Prepaid Debit Cards

If you aren't comfortable with the idea of carrying a lot of cash around, you can use prepaid debit cards, which you can purchase at any big-box store. As with the envelope system, you load the specific dollar amount you've determined to spend in a given month onto the card. Then, when making purchases in that area, you use the prepaid debit card for your spending in that area.

Two things to be aware of when it comes to prepaid debit cards: fees and expiration dates. Some card issuers charge initiation or recurring fees, making their cards a little more expensive than using cash. Shop around to find a no-fees card. Also, pay close attention to your card's expiration date; if the card expires with a balance, you may not be able to recover that money (at least not easily).

Budgeting Apps

There are also apps such as Mvelopes and Goodbudget that work as electronic cash envelopes to help you stay on budget.

Mvelopes lets you divide upcoming expenditures into separate virtual envelopes. This helps you in two ways. First, it allows you to make sure you have enough money to pay your recurring monthly bills. Second, it helps you keep track of how much you are spending in fluid budget areas such as groceries, entertainment, and eating out. Although you don't have to link to your bank account to use Mvelopes, it makes the system a lot easier to use as you don't have to enter each expense manually into the Mvelopes system. Mvelopes uses a secure encryption system to help protect your financial information. The Mvelopes app has three different programs to choose from: the free program, the Premier program, and the Coaching program (which comes with monthly one-on-one coaching sessions and other accountability tools).

Goodbudget also uses a virtual envelope system to help you budget your money. It allows you to target money for savings goals and sync the information you put in so that you can share it with a spouse or someone else. Goodbudget has two virtual envelope programs to choose from: the free program, which offers ten regular envelopes and ten additional envelopes for other budgeting purposes, and the Plus program, which offers unlimited envelopes and accounts as well as free email support. It also features a pie chart graphic that shows you what percentage of your money goes toward savings, spending needs, and spending wants.

Either of these online systems is a good alternative to a spreadsheet budgeting system if you like the online option better. The important part is that you are using some type of written or computer-based budget each month to help you monitor and manage where your money goes. In this way you can minimize waste, avoid going over budget, and maximize ERP savings.

Both of these systems require discipline. They require you to make a commitment that you're not going to exceed your predetermined spending in each area and take from other areas in your budget to make up the difference. But using a system such as the prepaid debit card system or cash envelope system will do wonders in keeping you on track with your budget. Since there's a finite amount on each card, you can't spend over what you've predetermined to spend via your budget without going through the trouble of finding other areas to take the money from. This type of discipline will allow you to maximize the amount of money you put into savings and investments each month and speed up your path to financial freedom.

The Secret Is in the Surplus

There's one secret to making a budget that will help you grow wealth quickly: have as much money as possible left over at the end of the month. The lower your expenses, the more money you'll have at the end of the month.

The fastest way for you to reach the magic number that will allow you to retire early is to track every penny and be conscious of every financial decision you make and how it affects your future. You've got to know that whatever you spend on frivolous things that don't really bring value to your life will push back your retirement date. We're going to talk more about this in Chapter 4 when we discuss opportunity cost, but for now, start working to view unnecessary expenses as a roadblock to growing wealth.

Understanding Your Net Worth

Do you know what your current net worth is? Simply defined, it's the sum total of your assets minus the sum total of your liabilities. Assets are everything you own, from your house down to your dining room table. But for the purposes of defining your net worth, you'll only count larger value assets that can be easily valued. Liabilities are the amounts you owe. The difference between the two equals your net worth. This can be positive (if you own more than you owe) or negative (if you owe more than you own).

Assets – Liabilities = Net Worth

Here are some examples of assets:
- House
- Land
- Retirement accounts (including 401(k)s and IRAs)
- Brokerage account
- Savings accounts and certificates of deposit (CDs)
- Cars, boats, and other valuable toys

Here are some examples of liabilities:
- Credit card debt
- Mortgage
- Car loans

- Payday loans and personal loans
- Student loans
- Outstanding medical bills

Knowing your net worth will give you a clear picture of your current financial situation. This will help you understand how prepared you currently are for early retirement. It can guide you as you make decisions about what financial moves you need to make before you retire. For instance, if you have a negative net worth, you may decide that you need to downsize your home or sell your newer, more expensive cars for less expensive cars. Decisions such as these will help you reach your early retirement goals.

THE IMPORTANCE OF 401(K)S

Even though you can't use 401(k) monies for the purposes of early retirement, it's important to consider investing in your company's 401(k) plan, especially if your employer offers a matching contribution. These funds will become an important part of your financial picture when you're able to start taking distributions from them later on in your life.

Which Retirement Funds Work for ERP?

Pension plans and 401(k)s are an important part of planning for retirement, but it's important to be careful about using them to plan for early retirement. Since the funds in 401(k)s and pensions are not available for withdrawal in early retirement without a tax penalty, it's smart to plan for your early retirement years as if those accounts don't exist. You must be fifty-nine-and-a-half to withdraw money from a 401(k) account without incurring at least a 10 percent tax penalty (on top of the income taxes you'll have to pay on every dollar you take out), and most pension plans don't allow you to begin receiving checks until at least age fifty-five, and in some cases age sixty-five. Check with your pension plan's fund manager or your employer to find out specific details on withdrawing from your pension plan.

Roth IRAs are another valuable retirement investing tool. The money you contribute to a Roth IRA isn't immediately tax deductible (like traditional IRAs and 401(k) contributions are), but the earnings grow and you can withdraw them completely tax-free (as long as you follow the rules). To date, those up to age fifty can contribute $5,500 per year to a Roth IRA vehicle, and those fifty and above can contribute $6,500 per year. Income phase-outs for Roth IRA contributions start at $118,000 for single tax filers and $186,000 for married tax filers, making it a great retirement investment for those in lower and middle income class brackets. It is important to remember that Roth IRA *earnings* usually cannot be withdrawn without tax penalty before age fifty-nine-and-a-half *and* until the account has been open for at least five years (though some exceptions apply, such as money to be used for first-time home purchases). However, you can withdraw the *contributions* you made to your Roth at any time with no tax hit whatsoever. Remember that "contributions" are the monies you added personally to your Roth IRA, whereas "earnings" constitutes the investment growth the fund earned over time.

CAN I DO BOTH?

As long as you meet the individual eligibility requirements for each (which may include limits on your income), you can fund both a

401(k) and a Roth IRA at the same time. However, the contribution limits of $5,500 per year for those under 50 and $6,500 per year for those 50 and over still apply, whether you are contributing to a traditional IRA, a Roth IRA, or a combination of the two.

Increasing Your Net Worth

Now it's time for you to figure out your current net worth. Stop here and create your net worth sheet using the form at the following website: http://wellkeptwallet.com/net-worth/.

What did you find? Is your net worth a positive or a negative number? Whatever it is, don't worry; it can be improved. The main goal you'll have as you work toward early retirement is to make sure that your net worth is consistently increasing.

You can do two main things to help this happen. First, you can find ways to make extra money to invest. Second, you can work to reduce or pay off debt. We'll talk more about how to do this in Chapter 5. Just know that the higher your net worth is, the closer you are to being able to retire early.

Growing Your Wealth for Early Retirement

In addition to saving by cutting expenses, you can also fund your planned early retirement by growing your wealth. There are three main options for growing wealth:

- Investing in real estate

- Investing in the stock market
- Building a business

Which of these routes is best for you based on your personality and your skill sets? We'll discuss all three of these in much more detail in Chapter 7. For now let's go over some of the basic things you might want to ask yourself as you decide which of these investing routes is the right fit for you and/or your spouse.

Real Estate Investing

Real estate investing is a great way to grow wealth, but it's not for everyone. Owning rental properties can require a hands-on approach and will take time out of your day as you collect rent, repair properties, work with tenants, etc. Some of the questions you might ask yourself before jumping into real estate investing are:

- Am I handy with things around the house?
- Do I like doing home maintenance and repair?
- Do I want to spend my retirement years caring for properties and working with tenants?

You can also hand off the management of your rental properties to a property management company, but this will eat into your monthly profit since you'll be paying them a fee. Take that into account when you're looking for properties to buy and analyzing their probable return on investment.

Risks Involved with Real Estate Investing

Real estate investing is not without its risks. Housing values can drop, for example, and periods of vacancy do happen. One thing to keep in mind when considering investing in rental properties to fund your ERP is that cash flow is more important than the value of the property. If housing values drop but you're still renting out your property, the drop in value does not have a direct effect on your ERP. A long period of vacancy, however, will affect your plan. That's why it's important to include a buffer within your rental income property margin, one that will have some money going directly into a separate savings account to cover periods when you're in between tenants. Having a separate emergency fund for your rental properties will help reduce monetary impact as you work to get new tenants. The emergency fund will also help with sudden large expenses such as replacing a broken furnace or putting on a new roof.

Stock Market Investing

Stock market investing is also one of the more popular ways people can make money to reach financial independence, but you need to decide if investing in the market is right for you.

Ask yourself:

1. What is my comfort level/risk tolerance? Can I handle the ups and downs of the market?

To get a clearer idea of what your risk tolerance is, take this quiz from Bankrate.com: www.bankrate.com/investing/quiz-what-is-your-risk-tolerance/.

Here are some of the questions you might ask yourself when working to determine your risk tolerance:

- How do I handle unexpected money? Do I save it or spend it?
- If the stock market tumbles, do I sell immediately, hold out for recovery, or invest more?

- When contributing money to my investments, do I prefer to invest in high-risk/high-return vehicles, low-risk/low-return vehicles, or a combination of the two?

Your answers to these and similar questions will help you decide where to invest your early retirement money. Those who choose the safest answer to the questions I posed above generally have a low tolerance for risk; those who choose the more daring answers generally have a high tolerance for risk.

2. What do I know about the different types of stock market investing?

How familiar are you with the different types of investments? Do you prefer buying individual stocks or investing in mutual funds or exchange-traded funds (ETFs)? Do you have the knowledge to make investing decisions on your own or would you be better off hiring a financial adviser?

3. Will I have enough money saved to survive a long-term downturn of the market?

Although in the long run the stock market is a profitable investment, market downturns do happen. As you prepare to retire early, it would be wise to consider adding a financial buffer in your investment account for any market downturns. A short market downturn likely would not affect your early retirement plans; however, one that takes three years or longer to recover from could make a significant impact on your early retirement income, especially if the crash happens close to your projected early retirement age.

As with real estate investing there are professionals who can help you invest your money in a way that matches your goals and your risk tolerance. However, it's important to be sure those professionals know what they're doing and to keep an eye on the fees you're paying them. High investment management fees can hinder the growth of your investments and delay your early retirement date. Many investment firms are now offering low-cost investment options that are managed by robo-advisers. These are essentially online investment tools that provide automated, algorithm-based management of investment portfolios (more on robo-advisers in Chapter 7). Because robo-advisers do not need to involve human management of the investment (beyond the initial setup) the costs to investors are much lower.

You need to keep inflation in mind when determining your fully funded early retirement plan numbers. Three percent per year for inflation is a good average to use as you calculate how much money you will need. Keep in mind that after retiring you'll have to pay at least some income taxes on your investment earnings and withdrawals, so you need to factor that in as an expense when you are creating your postretirement budget and determining the bottom-line amount you'll need in income and investments before you retire. Realize that the stock market has had significant downturns in the past, most recently with the Great Recession in 2008. However, note that over any ten-year period, the market has found a way to recover.

The examples I use here are based on a conservative, diversified portfolio. They don't apply to individual stock purchases or to day-trading. In fact, I suggest staying away from both of these investment options. Instead, go with solid-performing investment options that minimize risk. Index funds and other mutual funds with a proven long-term history of solid performance are the best choice (see Chapter 7 for more on index funds and mutual funds). Any other options involve a large amount of risk that could result in big losses. Just stay with tried-and-true profit-yielding investments such as index funds and other solid investment options (we will discuss these in more detail later in Chapter 7). Your goal as you gain wealth for early retirement should be "slow and steady wins the race."

That is why it is important to base your ERP on a low withdrawal rate, so that you minimize the risk of running out of money. As I've mentioned before, accounting for potential healthcare costs as you determine your target ERP amount is important as well. Expensive medical conditions such as Alzheimer's that require long-term care can diminish savings and investment accounts quite quickly.

Building a Business

Starting a business might be a way for you to invest your earnings toward early retirement as well. If you are inventive, resourceful, or love to solve problems, you may be able to create a business that will allow you to produce income. Alternatively, you can invest in a business that someone else creates and gain income that way. A profitable business can be a lifelong asset that could eventually fund your lifestyle or be available to sell if the numbers make sense. You have more control than if you invest in the stock market. For instance, you can cut your costs for your business, hire new employees, etc. Also, during recessions some businesses do even better—e.g., dollar stores, mechanic shops, etc.

When considering using business ventures to fund your ERP, it's important to do thorough research. Since a large percentage of all new business start-ups fail, you'll want to be sure that any business you are investing in involves a potential market that has staying potential over the long term. Fads and "the next big thing" are not generally the way to go when investing in businesses for the long haul.

As you can see, earning enough money to retire early is possible. There are risks involved with all of these options, but done right they'll help you get to early retirement much faster than putting your money into a savings account at a bank. We'll talk in depth about all three of these ideas in Chapter 7. For now, keep them in the back of your mind and be thinking about which of the three might be best for you.

As you read through the remainder of the book, continue to work on discovering which wealth-growing routes are most appealing to you, and think about the different ways you can formulate your ERP. Although your plan doesn't have to evolve continually, keeping a close eye on your personalized plan will help you identify when a part of the plan can be adjusted to better meet your goals.

CHAPTER 3

Making the Most of Your Income

Let's be clear: when it comes to having the cash to retire early, it is not about how much money you make; it's about what you do with that money. In the previous chapter we talked about the importance of increasing the amount of money you have left over at the end of the month (your surplus) by reducing your expenses. Making the most of your income means maximizing your monthly surplus, having a plan for the extra money you have at the end of every month, and being consistent about working that plan.

The reason so many people fail to achieve financial independence is because the trajectory they're on is a wealth-reducing path instead of a path that leads toward growing wealth. While the wealthy are spending their cash on income-producing assets such as real estate or private companies, the majority of people often spend money on assets that depreciate over time such as boats, cars, and ATVs.

If you want to go from paycheck-to-paycheck living to a financial situation that allows you to retire early, you have to change your mindset regarding your money and how you spend it. You have to start learning to think like financially secure people and avoid the short-term thinking that sends most people into a life of financial mediocrity.

What the Wealthy Know That the Rest of Us Don't

It's easy to see how people can end up with the wrong assets for building wealth. Society and the media tempt us to keep up with the Joneses. Whether it is on television, in magazines, or in stores, they sell us the illusion that if we have the newest and best of everything, life will be great. We read ads and see commercials of near-perfect people having the time of their lives with their new car, their new smartphone, or their designer clothes. What they don't show is the real-life story of those who try to live this type of lifestyle without a financial plan. They don't show the struggles of the 46 percent of Americans who are living paycheck-to-paycheck. They don't show the pain of bankruptcy that plagues the people who can no longer keep up the facade. Those who are financially secure, however, know differently.

The people who achieve financial freedom don't fall for the lie that stuff equals happiness. They understand that money better serves them by providing freedom.

The question you need to ask yourself is, who do you really want to be like?

- Your neighbor buys everything new and from the outside it looks like everything is great. In reality he and his family are drowning in debt, living paycheck-to-paycheck, and he and his wife are struggling in their marriage. Do you want to be that guy?
- Another neighbor is frugal in his habits. He and his spouse drive older, used cars, and their kids do chores around the neighborhood to earn extra money. They don't buy a lot of stuff, and when something breaks they try to fix it before replacing it. But

they seem on sound financial footing, and they've told you they plan to retire in their forties. Do you want to be that guy?

Don't be fooled by appearances, by marketing, or by the stories you read on Facebook about the guy you graduated from high school with who has an awesome life where nothing ever goes wrong. These pictures never show the whole truth. The fact is that "stuff" won't make you happy, not when you're faced with making monthly payments on that stuff for five, six, seven, or more years. Choose instead to take the path less traveled and do things your own way.

Steps to Minimize Your Expenses

Chances are that right now you're not on a trajectory to achieve financial independence. You're likely going to have to cut your expenses, increase your income, or both if you want to change your course and start growing some serious wealth. The first step to changing your financial path comes by choosing to not give in to this idea that everything in your life needs to look and be perfect. It's okay if your car isn't brand-new, your cell phone isn't the latest version, or your furniture doesn't match. Don't be concerned with perfection—instead focus on being okay with the cracks in your driveway and the chip in your countertop, knowing that you're trading the desire for perfection for a life of freedom.

Reducing Expenses

In the last chapter we talked a lot about the value of reducing expenses. You should now have a budget in place that shows you what you are spending in any given month. You should have also gone through the exercise of figuring out what are needs and what are wants.

It is important to analyze your budget on a regular basis. Don't just set it and forget it. Take some time each month to go over the upcoming month's expenses. Look at your budget with your ERP in mind and decide which "wants" you are willing to live without for the freedom of financial independence. Are you willing to reduce the amount of times you eat out during the month or cut restaurant visits altogether? Are you willing to start brown-bagging it for lunch?

What about limiting clothes shopping and just living with what you already have? Or living with your worn-out or out-of-style furniture for another five years?

You can have the same discussion about your "needs" list. For the sake of financial freedom, would you be willing to sell the car that is costing you $350 every month and buy a used car for cash? Even buying a car with a payment that's half as much as you spend now will help you to retire faster. Or maybe you can sell one of your cars and become a one-car family, using public transportation or carpooling.

What about reducing necessities such as insurance costs? Have you shopped around for homeowners and car insurance rates lately? Can you find a lower rate and bank the extra cash you save every month by switching carriers?

When was the last time you checked around for cell phone service plans? There are companies out there such as Republic Wireless and Consumer Cellular that charge a fraction of what most big-name companies charge. How much more cash would you have to invest in your ERP if you switched to a lower-priced cell phone plan?

Trimming Your Housing Expenses

Let's talk a bit more about reducing housing expenses. In the last chapter we talked a little bit about right-sizing your house. Here's an example of how right-sizing can put you on the fast track to early retirement.

Suppose there's a family of four living in a four-bedroom, 3,000-square-foot single-family home. Where I live in Arizona, you can get a house of that size for about $420,000 if you're moving to a nicer area of town. A $420,000 home purchase price with 10 percent down, a thirty-year loan, a 4 percent loan interest rate, and a loan balance of $378,000 would mean a mortgage payment of $1,804.63 (which doesn't include mortgage insurance, homeowners insurance, or property taxes).

In my own Arizona neighborhood you can get a four-bedroom, 1,800-square-foot house for around $215,000. If you put 10 percent down, that would mean that your mortgage payment on a thirty-year note at that same 4 percent interest rate would be $923.80.

That's a difference of $880.83. What would happen to your ERP if you had an extra $880.83 each month to invest?

If you invested that $881 every month for twenty years, at an ROI of 8 percent, you'd have an additional $504,513 in your investment account (this doesn't account for any taxes you'd owe on the earnings). That kind of cash can make the difference in just how early you can trade in the nine-to-five job for being your own boss.

This is the power behind right-sizing your house. As you assess your housing needs, it's important to think long term and decide what's more important to you: having a big, fancy house or having the freedom to be able to live your life on your terms.

Nearly every expense can be reduced in some way. You just need to be willing to do the work to find out how to live life on less.

How to Increase Your Income

If you're making minimum wage, it's going to be very difficult to reach financial independence. If your income is too low for you to be able to save any serious money, you need to look for ways to increase it.

Bringing more income into your home will help you reach your ERP goals faster. What avenues are available for you to do this? Most people choose one of three ways to make more money so they can reach the completion of their ERP sooner.

Make More Money in Your Current Job

Are there ways you could be making more cash at your current full-time job? Can you work overtime? Apply for a higher-paying position? Ask for a pay increase? Talk with your boss about ways that you can benefit the company and increase your income at the same time. Ask him or her how you can improve your performance and advance within the company. Be honest about the fact that you're looking to increase your income. Ask about other opportunities within your department or within the company and explore what steps you would need to take in order to qualify for those opportunities.

Be willing to take the initiative to learn in-demand skills that would help you excel at your job or that would benefit the company. If your job performance has been exceptional, don't be afraid to ask for a raise outright. When doing that, be sure to have a solid list of reasons why you deserve a raise. Make your boss aware of all of the ways you've been going above and beyond your position's required qualifications and present a good case for why you deserve a raise.

If there are no opportunities for increasing your income at your current job, should you consider moving to a company with better opportunities for advancement? Don't make this move without serious thought, but it might be something to contemplate if you're at a dead-end job that offers no room for advancement.

Take a Second Job

What about working part-time at a different company? You could find a position doing something similar to what you do now or get a job in a completely different field. Your second job can be doing anything from delivering pizzas, to cleaning homes and businesses, to being on staff as a hotel housekeeper.

You can work evenings and weekends as a waitperson at a local restaurant or do stock work or customer service for a nearby store. The choices for part-time jobs are available if you're willing to sacrifice some time now for the sake of financial independence later. Here are some ideas for some of the top second jobs available for full-time workers:

- Bartender
- Hotel or resort desk clerk
- Warehouse shipping and receiving clerk
- Customer service representative
- Janitor
- Delivery service driver
- Fitness instructor
- Retail sales associate
- Restaurant server
- Pizza or restaurant delivery driver

If the thought of working an additional part-time job seems overwhelming, remember that it only has to be temporary. Set an income goal for your second job and then, when your income goal is met, go back to just working nine-to-five.

Side Hustles

Owning your own business doesn't have to be a full-time job. When you're working for yourself to make extra cash, this is commonly referred to as a "side hustle." You can make a side hustle out of just about any skill. What are you good at? What do you enjoy doing? What are some ways you like to help other people?

If you're great at math and like kids, you can start your own tutoring business, advertising on local store bulletin boards or at school- or kid-centered events. If you like doing lawn work you can start a lawn-care business on the side.

Are you good with computers? Start a computer repair business. Do you have a knack for writing? Start a freelance writing business. Blog owners and company owners are constantly looking for someone to write blog articles and other content for their site.

SIDE HUSTLE EXERCISE

If you're interested in getting a side hustle, take an hour or two to write down what your talents and skills are, and what types of work you enjoy doing. Then figure out how you can use those skills, talents, and interests to create a side hustle that would bring in some extra cash. You should easily be able to come up with two, three, or four ways that you can earn some extra side hustle money that will help increase your income and get you to your ERP goals faster.

There are many ways for a person to make money by starting a small business. For instance, I know a guy who paid off over $50,000 worth of consumer debt in just seven months. Part of the way he earned that money so fast is that he started a business cleaning pools at night and on weekends.

Or check out Steve's story. Steve sharpens barber shears for $50 apiece. A shear-sharpening machine can cost as little as $199. Steve made his money back in the first weekend of his side hustle, and it's been nearly all profit from there.

There is no free lunch. Side hustles take time and effort. You have to find clients and build relationships with them. You have to prove yourself as a valuable asset to those potential clients.

In Steve's case, he has to go to the barbershops, pick up the shears, take them home, sharpen them, and then drop them off again. He probably takes some time in each shop to make small talk with the barbers. He might even join them outside of work for social reasons. The barbers keep coming back to Steve to get their shears sharpened for two reasons: first, he does great work; second, they like him.

If you're going to have a successful side hustle, you're going to have to treat it like the business that it is. You have to work to be one of the best in your field. Take the time to polish your skills, run your business with integrity and honesty, and give your clients service that they'll be happy to pay you for.

The Power of Blogging

Blogging is another way to create a long-term income, but it takes time and effort to establish a money-making blog. My own blog, *Well Kept Wallet*, makes $5,000–$10,000 every month. A lot of the income from my blog is passive income. Passive income is different from active income in that passive income requires little to no work to obtain, whereas active income requires that you work to get it. Since my blog already contains articles that have affiliate links in them for which I get paid for if readers follow those links, the money earned from those affiliate links no longer requires work on my part and is "passive" income. Income gained from working a part-time job is "active" income. However, it took me seven years of hard work writing articles and working to establish a loyal readership and form profitable affiliate relationships with companies that benefit my readers. Affiliate relationships are those formed with companies that pay people commissions to sell their products. For instance, one of the services I advertise on my blog is Personal Capital, a budgeting and investment firm. If someone clicks on a link to Personal Capital through my blog and opens an account with them, I get a commission.

On my blog I teach readers two main things: ways to build their wealth and ways to build their own side business. When I come across a service or product that has the potential to benefit my readers, I share a link to the business in an article where it makes sense. I then promote the articles on social media outlets such as Facebook, Pinterest, and Twitter and work to grow my readership by sharing tips and resources. The more interesting and helpful content I produce, the more people read my blog. The higher the readership, the higher the number of people who will click on the links I put in my articles, which results in a higher income for me each month.

If you have a lot of valuable information you could share with interested readers, blogging might be a way for you to make money, but know that marketing is key. Once you start your blog you need to get out into the blogging community, get to know other bloggers who write about similar topics, and be a source of help and support for them. As you do that your blog will become more recognized and you'll have more opportunity to grow readership and subsequently increase your income.

Penny Wise, Pound Foolish

It's important to have a balance when it comes to reducing expenses and increasing income. Don't be penny wise and pound foolish. For instance, if you spend an hour cutting coupons worth $10 when you could have earned $100 during that hour from side hustle work, then you've essentially lost money.

In order to avoid those types of mistakes, look for ways you can reduce expenses and increase income that will have long-term effects. Cutting cable or satellite TV is one of the ways to reduce expenses for the long term. It takes a five-minute phone call to cancel your cable TV subscription, but you'll save $100-plus dollars every month for as long as you go without it.

Don't Try to Keep Up with the Joneses

In the beginning of this chapter we talked about the impact media and advertising has on a person's willingness to keep at his or her ERP goals. If you can avoid falling into the trap of needing "new and shiny" things, you can reach your goal of early retirement much faster. Let's look at two different couples and their money. One couple fell for keeping up with the Joneses, and one couple didn't.

Case Study: Ashley and Brandon Keep Up with the Joneses

Ashley and Brandon love new and shiny things. They drive the best cars (new off the lot, of course) and live in an upscale house. Brandon and Ashley live large. They go to fine restaurants on date night, take international vacations, and visit Disney World every year with their two kids. They and their children dress in designer clothes and the kids have whatever toys they desire. They have the latest and greatest in technology and gadgets. Their kids are involved in every available activity and their schedule is jam-packed, leaving them little time for home-cooked meals. Their lifestyle eats up Brandon's $150,000 annual income fast. There's no money left over for savings, and Brandon is putting only 1 percent into his employer-sponsored 401(k) account. Even though Brandon's employer matches 401(k) contributions up to 3 percent, Brandon says they "just can't afford" to make bigger contributions until he starts making more money.

For many months Brandon and Ashley have been struggling to keep up with the house payments, the car payments, and the credit card bills. Fights about money and about who's spending what on what happen often. If a car repair or other financial emergency comes up, it has to go on the credit card, as the couple has no emergency fund savings.

Ashley and Brandon's story is all too common in this world where so many Americans live paycheck to paycheck. Now let's look at another couple. (Remember, these case studies illustrate *possible* personal financial circumstances.)

Case Study: Chris and Brittany Pave Their Own Path

Chris and Brittany strive not to focus on keeping up with the Joneses, but it is not easy. Many of their friends own upscale houses and drive newer, luxury cars, but Chris and Brittany have a dream: financial independence.

They bought a nice house in a decent area of town. It doesn't have granite countertops or cherrywood, but it's beautiful and is the right size for their family of four. Most importantly the house payment, which is on a fifteen-year note, only takes up about 20 percent of their take-home pay.

Brittany and Chris make the same $150,000 as Brandon and Ashley, but they spend their money much differently. They drive older, reliable used cars, which they can afford to buy with cash. Their annual vacations consist of a week at Chris's parents' cabin or visiting a nearby waterpark with the kids.

They get most of their clothes from big-box stores, thrift stores, or garage sales. They eat out once a month at their favorite, inexpensive family restaurant. The kids get to choose one sport or activity to be involved in each year.

The payoff for living a life of thriftiness has been big. At thirty-five, Chris has nearly $200,000 in his 401(k), even though he's never put in more than 3 percent of his annual pretax income. He started contributing when he got his job at age twenty-two, and the 100 percent employer match and the gift of time have made his retirement account grow nicely. His portfolio holds 70 percent equities and 30 percent bonds, which earned a 7 percent annual return (after 401(k) fees) to get to the $200k number. (The annualized return on the Standard & Poor's, or S&P, 500 during the period from January 2004 to December 2016 was 7.71 percent.)

Chris and Brittany have also been putting aside money to buy real estate rental properties. They've been saving 25 percent of his gross income for the past ten years and have been able to pay cash for three fixer-upper, single-family rental homes in their lower cost of living area. After paying cash and doing the renovations themselves with money used from their monthly living expenses, all three houses are rented out and their total incoming cash from the rental properties, after expenses, is $3,000 a month. The couple also has a $50,000 emergency fund.

Chris could retire from his full-time job now, but he wants to work another five years so that he and Brittany can save more money for an extra financial cushion and potentially to buy more rental properties.

The two couples in these case studies have the same income, but they've handled that money very differently. Their attitudes about money are totally different. Brandon and Ashley have no plans for being debt-free and no plans for how they'll pay for life in retirement. They're living the YOLO (you only live once) lifestyle and assume that "somehow" the future will take care of itself.

Brittany and Chris have traded in the YOLO lifestyle for a secure financial future that includes early retirement. To this couple, it's been well worth the sacrifice of material things so that they can see their dream of financial freedom come true.

Avoiding YOLO

I've seen the power of avoiding the YOLO lifestyle in the people around me. There was an older friend of my family whom I knew pretty well. This guy never made more than $30,000 a year in his life, but when he passed away he had a net worth of close to $1 million. He invested a small amount of each paycheck, mostly in dividend-paying blue-chip "dinosaur" stocks (shares of companies considered to be the most secure and reliable) that had a long-term steady history of growth and profits.

BLUE-CHIP STOCKS

Follow this link to a chart listing some of the more popular blue-chip stocks and their dividend payout amounts: www.dividend.com/dividend-stocks/dow-30-dividend-stocks.php.

Dividends are typically paid out quarterly or annually, so don't expect to get a payout every month from each stock you own. You may be able to invest in several dividend stocks that pay out on different schedules, for more steady cash flow. Before you retire,

---

it is worth considering reinvesting those dividend payouts back into your account so that your investment will grow that much faster (you'll still have to pay taxes on the dividends, though, even if you reinvest them). Then when you actually retire, you can discontinue reinvesting so that you can live off the dividend income.

On top of that, whenever a need arose, he was generous in supporting causes that were important to him. One time he even gave me a really nice older used car with low mileage. He didn't sell it to me; he just handed over the keys and signed off the title. He could do stuff like this—and did it often—because he avoided the lure of "new and shiny" and focused on financial security.

You may have read about the story of Ronald Read. Like my older friend, Read never made much money. He worked for years pumping gas. He also worked as a maintenance worker and janitor at a big-box store. When Read died at the age of ninety-two, his loved ones were astonished to learn that he had a net worth of nearly $8 million.

Read invested largely in blue-chip stocks with a solid history. He lived a frugal lifestyle, refusing to get caught up in the new-and-shiny trap. Obviously his frugality and persistence paid off. Although he left some money to family, the majority of his holdings went to improve services at a local hospital and library. He wanted to make an impact—and he did—on the lives of the thousands of people who visit the library and get services at the hospital.

The better you manage your money, the faster you'll be able to retire early. Make a choice to trade in the new-and-shiny lifestyle for the freedom of being able to live your life the way you want. Make the most of your income, and your efforts will repay you by giving you financial independence.

CHAPTER 4

Opportunity Cost and How It Affects Wealth

Opportunity cost is a benefit you could have received but sacrificed in favor of doing something else. By that definition, it doesn't sound like that big a deal—until you start running the numbers.

Every day people make choices about how they spend their money. They choose to have lunch out daily or to brown-bag it. They choose to buy coffee at the big-name coffee shop or to bring coffee from home. They choose to drive new cars with big payments or to drive quality, paid-for used cars.

These daily choices—both the big and the small—have a huge impact on whether or not you will have the cash you need to retire early. It's easy to think that $5 a day on coffee isn't a big deal to your long-term wealth, but once you check the math you'll find a different story. I don't want to suggest that giving up your daily latte will, in and of itself, enable you to retire early. Rather I want to point out the *combined* impact of all these smaller choices.

Where the Money Goes

Before we talk about how big an impact purchases can make on your ERP, let's look at what people are spending their money on so I can give you an idea of why retiring early seems out of reach for so many.

Following are just a few examples of what people in America spent their money on in 2015:

- $277.3 billion on new cars
- $53.3 billion on glassware, tableware, and household utensils
- $30.5 billion on books
- $77.2 billion on jewelry
- $133.3 billion for off-premise alcoholic beverages
- $300.2 billion on clothes
- $127 billion on gambling
- $671.6 billion on meals and beverages purchased at restaurants, cafés, etc.
- $182.3 billion on membership clubs, sports centers, parks, theaters, and museums
- $107.9 billion on tobacco purchases

When you look at the spending numbers, it suddenly becomes clear why people are having such a hard time saving money. But what would happen to their finances if they diverted some of this cash into an early retirement investment account?

I'm going to share four examples—two using big purchases and two using small purchases—that can give you an idea of the impact of opportunity cost and how it can substantially impede your ability to retire early.

WHICH CAR PURCHASES ARE PEOPLE MORE LIKELY TO FINANCE?

Eighty-five percent of new-car purchases are financed, while only 54 percent of used-car purchases are financed.

The New-Car Purchase

According to Experian Automotive the average loan amount for a new-car purchase in the fourth quarter of 2016 was $30,621, a record high. The average loan term was sixty-eight months, and the average new-car loan interest rate was 4.74 percent.

If you took out a car loan for sixty-eight months at a 4.74 percent interest rate on a $30,621 loan, you'd have a payment of $514.37. At the end of the loan term you would have paid $34,977, including $4,356 in interest, and that doesn't even include the amount you contributed as a down payment.

Now let's calculate the opportunity cost on that car. We'll assume that you put 10 percent down on the car, for a total of $3,000, and now instead use that money to open an investment account. Next, we'll assume you made monthly contributions to that investment account that are equal to what your car payment would have been, every month for six years, and never took any money out of the investment account.

Follow the Investment Calculator link at Bankrate.com to determine how much money you'd have at the end of six years (four months longer than the loan term), before taxes, if you earned 8 percent returns every year. As you can see, by the time the six years are up, you would earn $51,645 by putting the money in an investment account rather than spending it on a new car.

Car Payments: A Way of Life

The really sad thing about these numbers is that many new-car owners make payments a way of life. Before their new car is paid off, they trade it in for another new car. So, in reality they're probably losing a lot more than $50,000 to opportunity cost. If they buy new cars on a continual basis, they could actually be giving up more than $1 million and potentially throwing away a chance at early retirement altogether…because they buy new cars every five or six years. That $1 million is based on the assumption that the car loan payment would have remained the same for the entire thirty-five years (which it probably wouldn't), and that no additional money was used for down payments.

These are the numbers that no one at the car dealership or at the bank talk about when they approve you for your new-car loan, but they will have a huge impact on whether or not your ERP plan will become a reality.

Smaller purchases won't have as big an impact on your ERP, but they still add up. Let's go over a couple of common smaller purchases and how they rank in terms of opportunity cost.

The Gym Membership Purchase

Gym memberships are common in today's world. However, they can cost a lot more than you might have bargained for when you look at them in terms of opportunity cost. Let's say you and your spouse join the local gym. You pay a $149 starting membership fee to join the gym and a monthly fee of $99 a month after that. How much are you losing in terms of opportunity cost for the sake of being able to work out in a crowded gym where you have to wait for machines? At an 8 percent rate of return over a twenty-year period, you'd be losing out on more than $57,000. Not everyone will have a gym membership for twenty years, of course; however, lengthy memberships are becoming more common. This example shows how big an impact this can have on your ERP over the long term. What's worse, according to StatisticBrain, an astounding 67 percent of people who pay for gym memberships don't use them.

That $23k-plus you're spending on a couple of gym memberships could account for a few years of income, depending on your postretirement expenses. Instead of spending your money on a gym membership, invest the money and find other ways to work out. Some options for cheaper workouts include setting up a small gym at home and taking advantage of outdoor activities such as bicycling, hiking, and running. If you need more motivation, join a running club or find a partner who will keep you on track with your workout goals. Sign up for local charity runs or walks that commit you to training for a specific race date.

Small Purchases Can Really Add Up

Many times people get into financial trouble or have difficulty saving money and can't figure out why since they don't make big purchases such as furniture or new autos. The truth is that little, everyday expenditures can do just as much damage to your finances as big purchases can. Here are some examples:

- The $5 per day coffee shop habit can add up to around $1,300 per year.
- The $125 per month cable TV bill can add up to $1,500 per year.

- The $150 you spend on your monthly designer clothing splurge can add up to $1,800 per year.
- The $10 per day lunch at the local café near your job can add up to $2,600 per year.
- The $300 a month you spend on happy-hour trips and restaurant visits can add up to $3,600 per year.

Altogether, these seemingly small purchases add up to more than $10,000 per year. If instead you invest that $10,000 a year, contributing $833 every month, into a mutual fund earning 8 percent, you'll accumulate nearly $475,000 in only twenty years (before taxes, as long as you never take out any money).

Little purchases can add up to big opportunity cost losses if you let them.

The Lottery Ticket Purchase

In 2014 Americans spent $70.15 billion on lottery tickets.

How would breaking a lotto ticket habit affect your early retirement plan?

Let's assume you're spending $15 a week on various lottery tickets. If you chose instead to invest that money (an average of $65 per month) at 8 percent over forty years, you'd end up with $209,370 in your investment account.

Even if you're not planning to retire early, there are other ways you can avoid opportunity cost loss and change your or your family's future. For instance, what if instead of buying lottery tickets, you chose to invest that $65 every month for eighteen years so you could save it for your kid's college fund? At the end of eighteen years, assuming an 8 percent rate of return, you'd have $30,267.

What kind of an impact would that money have on your child's future? How much money would she save in interest payments alone if she had to take out $30,000 less in student loans? A $30,000 student loan taken out at a 6 percent interest rate over five years would cost nearly $5,000 in interest.

The Daily Coffee Shop Purchase

If you're like many people, you'll stop at the local coffee shop on your way to work and pick up a nice flavored mocha to start your day. If you're paying $5 per day five days a week for that mocha, you're spending roughly $100 per month. What would happen if you invested that money instead?

If, instead of spending that money on coffee, you'd invested that $100 a month at 8 percent for thirty years, you'd have $140,855 in your early retirement account (before taxes, if you never took out any money). Just that one move alone could have you well on your way toward an early retirement goal of $800,000.

Comparing Opportunity to Opportunity Cost

The opportunity cost of an expense is based on the idea that you *could have* invested that money instead. To figure out the opportunity cost of any expense, add the total cost of the expense itself plus any ROI you could have earned if the money had been invested. In other words, when you purchase something you don't just pay the cost of the purchase price. You pay for the lost profit you would have had if you had invested the money in a profitable venture instead of spending it on that particular item.

Let's take a look at two case studies of different spending styles: one couple who understands the impact of opportunity cost and one couple who doesn't.

Case Study: Courtney and Cody Spend Money

Courtney and Cody have been married for ten years and have two kids. Cody works as a financial analyst and Courtney works in interior design for a local remodeling company. Throughout their ten years of marriage, they've accumulated all the "stuff" that society says people need to be successful. They have a newer home, newer high-end cars, and buy designer clothes and household goods. They have a goal to save money to put their kids through college, but they just can't seem to find the money to save.

The family also loves to eat out and travel—especially internationally. Instead of saving for the kids' college tuition, they've been spending their money on taking one international trip annually. Over the past ten years, they've been to ten different countries including Japan, Ireland, Bora Bora, Switzerland, and Australia. Each trip costs them about $6,000, which averages out to $500 a month spending on international vacations alone. What's more, that doesn't include the credit card interest costs they rack up by not paying off their balance immediately.

Because Cody and Courtney aren't saving money on a regular basis, they put their vacations on a credit card that charges 16 percent interest but they do have the vacation paid off in one year. The problem with their plan is that as soon as they pay off one vacation, they charge another on a credit card. So they're paying an extra $532.68 in interest for each vacation as well. What would happen if they'd invested that $544.39 credit card payment (the monthly payment to pay off the $6k balance plus the monthly interest charge) each month for ten years instead?

If they invested $544.39 every month for ten years, and earned an annual ROI of 8 percent, after ten years was up they would have

$97,988. This money could potentially pay for both of their kids' college costs. At the very least, it would make a big dent in those costs.

Achieving early retirement is largely about making choices. When you choose to spend your money on one thing, you often choose to give up another. If you want to retire early, you need to identify your current spending choices and determine whether those choices are conducive to retiring early.

If those spending choices are not helping you move toward early retirement, they're moving you away from early retirement, and you need to decide whether or not those spending choices are worth giving up your goal of being able to retire early.

The ability to think long-term about your money and your spending choices is the hardest part of carrying out an ERP. It can be tough to give up the things you want now for things you want later, especially when "later" is fifteen or twenty years down the line. However, if you work to solidify what you truly want out of life, you'll likely find that those things you think you want now aren't nearly as important to you as the freedom to be able to retire early and have complete control over how you spend your days.

Let's take a look at another case study that shows how avoiding many of the "normal" purchases that people make today can impact one's ability to retire early.

Case Study: Eric and Alexandra Save and Invest

Eric and Alexandra have been married for ten years. Eric works as an internal auditor for a large company and Alexandra stays home with their son and daughter. When they were first house shopping, they thought about buying a large, upscale house like many of their friends. After all, Eric makes good money. They were looking at houses as high as $500,000 that came with all the bells and whistles they'd ever need.

Instead, they bought a $200,000 house. The house is modest but nicely updated thanks to years of improvements they've done themselves. They drive quality used cars they bought with cash. They take one annual vacation to a nearby bed-and-breakfast each year, and they spend very little on clothing and entertainment. Instead, they have friends over for a once-a-month game night or see free concerts at the local downtown park. When they need new clothes, they wait for sales, buy at big-box stores, and shop garage sales.

Eric and Alexandra's current house payment is $961.16 for their twenty-year loan with a 3.9 percent interest rate. They put down $40,000, a 20 percent down payment, on their 1,800-square-foot house. This means they don't have to pay private mortgage insurance (special insurance designed to protect mortgage lenders from borrower defaults) on top of their principal and interest payment. Their taxes on the house work out to $208 per month and homeowners insurance is $83 a month. Their average heat and electricity cost is $150 a month. Water usage runs $40 a month. They spend roughly $90 a month for maintenance and repair. In total the couple spends $1,532.16 a month to own and maintain their home.

If Alexandra and Eric had chosen to buy a $500,000 home with twice the square footage, their mortgage and home maintenance costs would look quite different. Their principal and interest payment would have been $2,262.92 because they would be paying a higher interest rate of 4.25 percent since they would have had to take out a thirty-year loan instead of a twenty-year loan so as to comfortably afford the payments. Because they only had $40,000 to put down, they also would have had to pay private mortgage insurance on the loan. Private mortgage insurance runs between 0.5 percent and 1 percent of the loan amount on an annual basis, so we'll average that out by saying their private mortgage insurance would have been 0.75 percent of their loan amount annually. This would add $287.50 to their monthly loan payment.

Because taxes, insurance, and utility costs are also higher for a bigger house, those numbers would change too. Their monthly property taxes in the upscale neighborhood where the expensive house was located would have been closer to $475 per month. The energy costs would have doubled too, to $380 a month for heat, electricity, and water usage, given that the bigger house had a seventy-gallon water heater as opposed to a forty-gallon water heater, and the master bathroom was equipped with a large, jetted tub. Insurance costs for the bigger house would also have been higher, estimated at roughly $150 a month. Maintenance and repair costs likely would've doubled too, to the tune of $180 a month.

So their estimated total monthly cost to own and maintain the bigger house would have been $3,735.42.

By choosing the smaller, more inexpensive house, they could be saving roughly $2,200 a month.

Let's lay this out in the form of a chart:

Comparison of Housing Costs		
	Actual House	**Larger House**
Mortgage interest rate	3.9%	4.25%
Monthly mortgage payment	$961.16	$2,262.92
Private mortgage insurance		$287.50
Homeowners insurance	$83	$150
Monthly property taxes	$208	$475
Heat, electricity, and water monthly usage	$190	$380
Maintenance and repair	$90	$180
Total	$1,532.16	$3,735.42

Because they chose the lower-priced house over the half-million-dollar house, each month for the past ten years they've been able to put what they saved by buying the smaller house, plus a little more each month—totaling $2,500—into an investment account that gains an 8 percent annual return. They hope to be able to retire by the time Eric turns forty, which is in seven years. So far, their plan is working and they have over $450,000 in their early retirement investment account.

If they keep investing $2,500 every month at this same rate for another seven years, they'll have more than a million dollars in their investment account and Eric will be able to move on to other opportunities for work or volunteering or whatever he and Alexandra choose.

These are the benefits that come with recognizing the losses that come via opportunity cost and making choices that will help you avoid opportunity cost losses and choose financial freedom instead. If you want to maximize your chances of success with your ERP, it's important to recognize the opportunity cost of every purchase you make, no matter how small.

CHAPTER 5

The Role of Fixed Debt

Fixed debt normally involves long-term structured loans, such as mortgages and car loans; it's also often referred to as installment loans. With fixed debt, your monthly payment is set, determined by your loan agreement. All of the loan terms are fixed: the loan amount, the length of the loan, the interest rate, and the monthly payment. (If you have an adjustable rate loan, your interest rate and loan payment may change periodically, and you would know that in advance.)

This type of debt is usually tied to asset purchases (such as houses and cars), education, and business loans. While many financial pros consider these types of loans "good debt," it can get in the way of early retirement dreams.

How Fixed Debt Impacts You

Fixed debts can potentially block or even crush your ERP goals in a number of different ways. The most prominent way fixed debt does this is that having fixed monthly debt payments takes away hundreds and sometimes thousands of dollars each month that could be used toward growing wealth. Second, the assets people purchase using fixed debt cost money to maintain, which means there is hidden spending for fixed-debt assets that increases the money you are taking away from your early retirement fund.

The general rule about debt is that it's best to only use debt to purchase an appreciating asset such as a home or business, but even then debt can be dangerous and must be used with caution. For those planning to go against the norm and retire early, even debts on appreciating assets can shatter ERP goals. For instance, an appreciating asset such as a home means that costs such as property taxes will likely increase as your home value increases. As the home gets older, more and more money will need to be spent on repairs. For instance, an air conditioner could go out and need to be replaced. Perhaps you will start having problems with the roof and need a new one. On the other hand, if you choose to rent instead of own, those costs will be eliminated, freeing up more money for your ERP. The main downside to renting is that you have a fixed cost that doesn't go away. If you own your home, after fifteen or thirty years your mortgage is paid off and you no longer need to make a monthly payment (plus, there are some beneficial tax breaks related to home ownership that help offset some of the costs). In addition, you now have a valuable asset that may be used later to provide for retirement income if needed.

Limiting Your Retirement Options

Fixed debt limits your early retirement options because it increases the amount of income you need to survive each month. That means your investment fund or postretirement income sources will have to be larger so that they can cover the monthly payments tied to your fixed debt. It will be easier to save $2,000 a month to live on postretirement than it will be to save for $2,000 a month in expenses plus another $2,000 a month to cover a house payment, taxes, insurance, maintenance, and repair costs. Adding such big numbers to your postretirement expenses means you have to increase your savings substantially, decrease your postretirement living expenses substantially, or both.

The Stress of Carrying Debt

Fixed debt can cause stress and pressure that can take your focus off your goals and distract you from getting where you want to be financially. The stress that comes with debt has also been known to cause physical symptoms in many people, such as anxiety and anxiety-related illness. Stress-related illnesses can come in the form of high blood pressure or migraine headaches, or as psychological illness such as depression or anxiety attacks. Avoiding fixed debt means you won't have to worry about whether or not you can make your monthly loan payments.

Debt and Opportunity Cost

As we discussed in the last chapter, debt can have a massive opportunity cost, causing you to waste money paid in interest to banks and lenders and diminishing the amount of compound interest you would have been able to accumulate had the money you're paying to lenders been funneled into investments instead. When you take on fixed-debt payments, you don't just lose the monthly payment you are paying to service the debt; you lose the compound interest that would have accrued had you invested that money each month instead.

What Is a Healthy Debt-to-Income Ratio?

In order to keep debt from debilitating your early retirement plans, it's a good idea to understand the basics of the debt-to-income (DTI) ratio, a key measure of your ability to repay your debt. When this ratio is too high, it can be more difficult to keep up with loan payments and put you at greater risk for default.

A low DTI ratio means you have more money to put toward your ERP goals. The less money you have going toward fixed-debt payments each month, the lower your DTI ratio, and that translates into a quicker path to early retirement because you have more money to save and invest each month.

Calculating Your DTI

Your debt-to-income ratio is calculated by dividing your total monthly debt payments by your total gross monthly income. For instance, if your gross monthly income is $5,000 and your total debt payments equal $2,000, your debt-to-income ratio is 40 percent ($2,000/$5,000 = 40 percent). If your gross monthly income is $4,000 and your total debt payments are $1,000, your debt-to-income ratio is 25 percent ($1,000/$4,000 = 25 percent).

Most mortgage lenders will allow a person with good credit to borrow up to 36 percent of their monthly gross income, but the numbers show that this could set the borrower up for financial failure. It certainly won't move you closer to the goal of early retirement. If you make $5,000 gross per month, you can qualify for mortgage payments of up to $1,800, but we have to remember that the formula used to calculate DTI is based on *gross* income. This means that the family with the $1,800 house payment isn't really bringing home $5,000 each month; it's probably closer to $4,000 per month after taxes and benefit deductions. That leaves them $2,200 a month for all other expenses—including property taxes and homeowners insurance, which are often added into the monthly mortgage payment, but are not included in that 36 percent DTI number. That can be tough to manage on, especially for families raising children.

The general rule when determining the best debt-to-income ratio for your family is this: the lower your DTI, the better. A lower DTI means you'll have more money to cover expenses and to invest toward early retirement. The higher your DTI, the further out your retirement date will be. Here is a more detailed way for you to assess how to have a healthy DTI number for the purposes of early retirement.

Debt-to-Income Ratios and Risk Factor

In an ideal world those working toward early retirement would aim for a 0 percent DTI. No monthly debt payments mean your annual cost-of-living expenses are without debt obligations that will eat up your postretirement monthly income.

The following worksheet will help you figure out your current debt-to-income ratio.

Debt-to-Income Ratio Worksheet	
MONTHLY INCOME NUMBERS	
Gross monthly income #1	_____
Gross monthly income #2	_____
Total gross monthly income	_____
MONTHLY DEBT OBLIGATIONS	
Monthly mortgage loan payment	_____
Auto loan payment #1	_____
Auto loan payment #2	_____
Other fixed loan payment #1	_____
Other fixed loan payment #2	_____
Credit card or other payment	_____
Credit card or other payment	_____
Total monthly debt obligations	_____
Total monthly debt obligations divided by total gross monthly income	_____ % DTI

How risky is your current debt-to-income ratio? Here is a break-down that will help you assess the risk level of your current DTI:

- Under 15 percent DTI: Good
- 15–25 percent DTI: Risky
- Over 25 percent DTI: Dangerous

If your current DTI ratio is at a dangerous level, higher than 25 percent, it's important to formulate a plan to pay off your debt as soon as possible. But even if your DTI is at a lower level, paying off your debts will improve your chances of a successful ERP. Now we'll go over the different types of fixed debt and how you can minimize their impact on your ERP.

Types of Fixed Debt

There are four main types of fixed debt: mortgage loans, auto loans, other fixed-debt loans (such as boat, cabin, or ATV loans), and student loans. All four of these can overtake your early retirement plans, but there are ways to avoid carrying these and all other types of fixed debt.

Real Estate

Your primary residence and/or vacation home is likely your largest source of fixed debt, and as such will probably have the biggest impact on your ERP. There are safer ways to use mortgage debt that will help preserve your early retirement plan.

Mortgage debt is generally considered "good" debt. Because you are buying an appreciating asset instead of a depreciating one (usually), mortgage debt is considered safer than many other types of debt. However, debt is still debt. If you are set on buying a house, consider these safer ways to use mortgage debt:

- **Consider right-sizing:** Instead of choosing a home based on the maximum amount your mortgage company will lend you or what others are buying, make sure you buy the home that is right for your family. For instance, you might qualify for a 4,000-square-foot mini-mansion, but is that truly what you need? Or will a smaller house that is half that size work for you and allow you to reach your goal of early retirement faster? Assess your true housing needs and buy the house that's right for your goals.

- **Put at least 20 percent down:** Putting at least 20 percent down means you can avoid having to pay private mortgage insurance, which can raise your mortgage payment by up to 1 percent of the loan value per month. A higher down payment also puts a bigger buffer between you and a housing market crash, helping reduce the risk that you'll be underwater on your loan and be stuck owing more than your house is worth. Another advantage of putting down at least 20 percent: it could make you eligible for a lower interest rate on your mortgage.

- **Consider a fifteen-year loan:** Choosing to buy based on qualifying for a fifteen-year loan instead of a thirty-year loan can save you hundreds of thousands of dollars in interest over the life of the loan—and get you mortgage debt–free in half the time. Keep in mind that fifteen-year loans usually come with much bigger monthly mortgage payments than thirty-year loans. They also come with lower interest rates, reducing the total interest you'll pay over the life of the loan even further. Let's look at the numbers.

Case Study: Charlie and Liz Get a Mortgage

Charlie and Liz are buying a house that will leave them with a $250,000 mortgage. If they get that $250,000 mortgage with a thirty-year term at 4 percent (and a monthly payment of $1,193.54), they'll pay $179,676.94 in interest if they don't pay off the loan early.

However, if they choose a fifteen-year term, their monthly payment will increase to $1,849.22, and they'll pay $82,865.67 in interest if they don't pay off the loan early. That's a difference of $96,811.27. (For this example, we'll use the same interest rate for both loans even though the fifteen-year loan would normally have a lower interest rate.)

Now let's look at that $96,000 in terms of opportunity cost. If Charlie and Liz were to invest that money over the course of fifteen years at an interest rate of 8 percent (assuming a contribution of $537.84 every month for fifteen years, and no withdrawals—the total interest savings divided by the 180 months of the fifteen-year loan), they'd have over $180,000 in the bank. So, by taking out a fifteen-year loan, and then putting the interest they would have paid for the additional fifteen years in investments (after the fifteen-year mortgage is paid off), Charlie and Liz add an additional amount of nearly $200,000 to their ERP fund.

If they were to continue investing that $537.84 for an additional fifteen years (for a total of thirty years), at the same 8 percent rate, they'd accumulate over $750,000.

This means that the opportunity cost of taking the thirty-year loan instead of the fifteen-year loan is $854,611.27, as Charlie and Liz would lose the $96,811.27 they paid extra in interest and the $757,800 they lost from not investing the interest savings over that thirty-year period. (Note that this model is based on fixed assumptions, offering one possible outcome.)

As you can see, just this one decision about your mortgage term can mean the difference between retiring early and not retiring early.

Paying Off Your Mortgage Early

If you already own your home and have a mortgage, paying off that mortgage early is vital to a successful ERP. Here are some ways to do that:

- Get a second job and put all extra income toward additional principal payments on your mortgage
- Switch to bimonthly mortgage payments (instead of monthly), which will result in one additional mortgage payment per year
- Refinance your mortgage with a lower interest rate to lower your payments, but continue to make the old, larger mortgage payment
- Eliminate discretionary spending for a period of time, putting all monthly savings toward extra mortgage payments
- Sell items you have around the house that you don't need and put the earned income toward your mortgage balance
- Put any unexpected income such as bonuses, tax returns, or monetary gifts toward paying down your mortgage

Every extra dollar you put toward paying off your mortgage faster will help you enter early retirement with a lower debt-to-income ratio and a healthier postretirement balance sheet.

Carrying a Mortgage Into Retirement

In my opinion it's best to enter early retirement mortgage-free. Having a debt obligation on your place of residence means you have to put a priority on those monthly payments because you need a place to live. Since house payments are usually quite large, the impact that a mortgage payment will have on your ERP can be pretty substantial.

However, if you're not planning to pay off your mortgage before you retire, here are some ways you can minimize the mortgage's impact on your postretirement financial situation:

- **Refinance to get a better interest rate:** Refinancing to a lower interest rate—and monthly payment—will make those payments more manageable and help you to pay off your mortgage faster, as long as you don't increase the remaining term on your mortgage. Check daily mortgage rates so you can lock in at a lower rate when one comes along.
- **Increase your targeted savings amount:** Another way to minimize the impact a mortgage payment has on your ERP is to increase your targeted ERP savings amount. Additional savings in your ERP can be used as a buffer to cover mortgage payments if need be.

Some people do carry mortgages into retirement, but the vast majority of those who retire early do so mortgage-free.

Auto Loans and Other Fixed Loans

Auto loans and loans for recreational vehicles or other purposes are another type of fixed loan that can have a negative impact on your ERP. Many people in today's world simply plan on always having a car payment, but that doesn't have to be the case.

In my family, my wife and I drive quality used cars—usually costing under $7,000—that we pay for with cash. We make this work for us by knowing what we want before we start looking, taking our time and shopping carefully, and keeping within our allotted car budget.

Our car purchase budget always includes an extra $1,000 for doing any necessary repairs that might come with buying a used car.

We're also very particular when it comes to what we're willing to spend our money on in the area of personal items. We keep our furniture for many years and don't upgrade or make home repairs that aren't truly necessary. For instance, the faucet on our kitchen sink has a chip out of the metal. The chip doesn't harm the performance of the faucet, but it is noticeable. People have remarked that we should replace the faucet, but we'd rather put that $300 toward paying off our mortgage. It doesn't make any sense to us to replace a perfectly functional faucet for the sake of appearance. Our financial goals are more important to us.

Having the same attitude when it comes to auto loans or other personal loans will help you fund your ERP faster. When you're faced with making a purchase, weigh it against the potential of reaching your early retirement goal and decide what is more important to you. That will help you make spending decisions more objectively.

Here are three steps you can take that will help you avoid car payments:

1. **Never buy new:** As I mentioned in Chapter 4, buying a quality used vehicle will help you save tens of thousands of dollars over the long term.

2. **Find alternative transportation options:** Most families today believe that having two cars is a necessity, but there are things you can do to survive with one car—or even no cars. Carpooling, using public transportation, or living in an area that is walking/biking friendly are all viable alternatives to owning a car.

3. **Negotiate well and pay cash:** Learn how to be a tough but fair negotiator when purchasing a vehicle. Paying cash will also give you more negotiating power.

Work the different avenues I've mentioned as you determine how you can minimize the financial impact of cars and other big-ticket items and avoid taking out auto or personal loans.

Student Loans

College is another area where people say it's not possible to fund your degree without student loan debt. In fact, the average college graduate from the class of 2016 has more than $37,000 in student loan debt.

Most students are encouraged to start college right out of high school. The danger with this is that very few people have a clear idea about what they want to do with their lives at age eighteen. In fact, only 27 percent of college graduates were working in their degree field according to a 2010 study. What's worse, a 2014 study showed that 51 percent of employed 2014 college graduates were working in fields that didn't require a degree at all.

These studies are a good reason to think carefully about how to best make college work for you, both from a career and a financial perspective.

After careful thought, depending on the field you want to work in, you may determine that you don't want or need to go to college. However, if you know that you want to go to college and are confident in your career choice, there are ways to minimize or avoid having student loan debt. Here are some suggestions.

Save the Money Before You Go

A person who is willing to work hard and save a large percentage of her or his income can save the money for tuition before going to college. By working full-time, minimizing expenses, and saving all that you can, paying cash for school is possible under certain circumstances. For instance, if you chose to delay college by three years, worked a full-time job that paid $17 per hour, and lived at home with your parents, minimizing rent and discretionary expenses (assuming that is an option), you could potentially save $60,000 toward college tuition.

Minimize College Costs

Reducing how much your college costs will help as well. There are several ways to do this:

- Take your first two years at a less expensive community college.
- Live at home with your parents instead of using on- or off-site college housing (if that is an option).
- Buy books and other supplies second hand.
- Test out of courses you know well using CLEP or other testing systems.
- Assess several different state and private college costs, taking into account grants and scholarships before you choose your school. It can often cost less to attend private schools because some have more scholarship and grant resources available.

BALANCING WORK AND STUDY

Make sure you'll have time to study and keep up with your classes when you take on a full-time or part-time job. It defeats the purpose of going to college if you have to retake classes because of your work schedule.

It's also a good idea to minimize your other expenses while you're in school. Many people go into debt while in college as a result of overspending in areas outside of school costs. Apartment rental costs, socializing, and shopping are all temptations for college students. Spend as little as possible when you're in college so that all the money you've saved or are earning can be used to pay for the degree itself.

Work Your Way Through School

Working part-time with a full-time school schedule—or full-time with a part-time school schedule—means you'll be earning cash to help pay for school as you go. This can help you reduce or in some cases eliminate the need for student loans.

Another thing to consider: look for a job at a company that will pay for your education. Some companies in certain industries will pay for college courses if they relate to your job. Getting a job at a company in your field that pays for college courses will allow you to get a free or partially free education as you work and earn money at the same time.

When Student Loans Might Pay Off

Sometimes student loans can be worth consideration. If you're earning a degree in law or medicine that will result in a high-paying salary, it may be beneficial to take out some of the money you need via student loans, provided you've used the tips above to minimize college costs and pay cash when possible.

The college you choose should be based in large part on whether the cost of attending can be recouped based on the starting salary of your chosen profession. Going to an expensive private college may make sense if you're entering a high-paying field that will allow you to pay off your student loans quickly, but that's not always the case. Often students focus on the school name on their diploma when many employers don't take that into consideration. That choice can leave students in financial ruin.

Case Study: Sarah's College Degree Dilemma

Sarah, who lives in New York City, wants to be a social worker. She's been accepted to several colleges, including Columbia University, a school she's always wanted to attend. Save for a $10,000 gift her parents worked hard to save and give her to put toward college costs, Sarah will be paying for school largely on her own.

Columbia University's current tuition and fee rate is $55,161 per year. This means that Sarah will pay over $220,000 just for tuition and fees alone if she chooses to attend Columbia. On a starting salary of just over $48,000 (the average starting salary for social workers in New York) it will take Sarah decades to pay off those student loans.

However, she has another choice. The University of Buffalo—a public university—offers the same degree in social work that Sarah could get at Columbia. The difference is in the cost. Tuition and fees at the University of Buffalo are $9,770 per year, meaning tuition and fees for her degree at the University of Buffalo would total $39,080, a far more reasonable amount to pay off in student loans if she isn't able to pay in cash as she goes. If Sarah was planning on obtaining a law degree, Columbia might be the better school, but you should weigh career salary against tuition costs before making a college choice.

No matter which college route you choose, it's important to pay off any student loans as soon as possible after you graduate and start working so that you aren't paying the opportunity costs of carrying student loans and their high interest rates for many years to come.

Refinance Student Loan Debt to Your Advantage

If you're already carrying student loan debt, refinancing to a lower rate and a shorter term may save you money and help you pay down your student loan faster. For instance, many private student loans charge interest rates as high as 9–12 percent. However, many of the lending institutions that specialize in refinancing private student loans charge much lower interest rates, sometimes as low as 3 percent (for adjustable rate loans).

Student Loan Forgiveness

The general rule is that student loans must be repaid even if you quit school before graduating, can't find a job in your field of study, or are unhappy with your field of study. However, in some circumstances you may be able to have at least a portion of your outstanding student loan balance forgiven, canceled, or discharged.

Also, in some cases, permanent disabilities may make a person eligible for student loan forgiveness. Finally, in very rare cases student loan debt may be discharged by bankruptcy—but this is a very difficult and complicated path, and it usually doesn't work for student loan debt.

How to Use Cash Instead of Debt

Paying for assets such as a home, car, or college degree with cash does take effort. However, it's not as difficult or impossible as it may seem. Here are some ideas for how you can pay cash for items you want and avoid carrying debt payments that will diminish your chances of retiring early.

To Buy a House

A great way to avoid debt and maximize your investment potential is to consider paying cash for a house. At first glance it sounds pretty outlandish to buy a house for cash unless you're looking at a serious fixer-upper. Let's look at a case study.

Case Study: Crystal and Kevin Pay Cash for a House

Crystal and Kevin, a married couple in their early twenties, decided that they wanted to buy a house. They planned on paying roughly $230,000 for their house (the median price for a home in the United States as of June of 2016). Kevin is a physical therapist. Crystal is a dental hygienist. They've decided to live off only Crystal's income in a small, rented studio apartment. That will allow them to pay extra on their student loans and save all of Kevin's take-home pay of $4,500 a month to purchase a home with cash. Crystal's take-home pay after taxes (and no other deductions) is approximately $3,500 per month. Their studio apartment costs them $800 per month. Living modestly, they can put $1,000 toward their student loans a month and use the remaining $1,700 a month to cover food, transportation, utilities, and their modest discretionary expenses.

They decided to put the money in a high-yield savings account earning 1 percent in order to avoid the risk of losing the money. After five years, they saved over $276,000, more than enough to cover the cost of a house in their price range, closing costs, and any needed repairs.

Paying cash for a home isn't as difficult as it seems for those willing to put in the effort. If, on the other hand, Kevin and Crystal had chosen to take out a mortgage on their $230,000 home, what would they have paid in interest?

If the couple had chosen a fifteen-year mortgage at a 4 percent interest rate with a 5 percent down payment, they would have paid $72,419.17 in interest over the life of the loan (this model does not include PMI, which they would have had to pay with a 5 percent down payment).

If Kevin and Crystal had taken out a thirty-year mortgage on the home at the same interest rate (though normally the rate on a thirty-year loan would be higher than that on a fifteen-year loan) and with the same 5 percent down payment (also without any PMI calculation), they would have paid $387,035.70 for their home after thirty years ($230,000 purchase price plus $157,035.70 in interest).

Instead, they paid no interest and moved into their home with no mortgage debt, allowing them to continue to funnel Kevin's $4,500 a month in take-home pay (and more as he received raises) into their early retirement account.

Starting over at that savings rate, Kevin and Crystal will have enough money in their investment account to retire in just fifteen years.

Although paying cash for a house does require patience, it can be done if you are willing to keep in mind the end result: financial freedom.

To Pay for College

It is also possible to pay cash for your college degree and avoid student loans altogether.

Let's look at a case study that shows how Holly might be able to pay cash for her degree instead of borrowing for it.

Case Study: Holly Goes to College

Holly wants to go to college to get a degree in elementary education from a school in her home state of Arizona. She has narrowed her choices to two Arizona schools: the University of Arizona and Prescott College. Here's what it will cost to get her degree from each of the two schools.

The University of Arizona's in-state tuition is $11,800 per year. This means that Holly's four-year degree will cost her $47,200 for tuition and fees. Prescott College is a private college that charges $28,228 per year. If Holly gets her four-year degree at Prescott, it will cost a total of $112,912 for tuition and fees.

Both of these colleges could leave Holly with a big student loan balance to pay after graduation. However, the University of Arizona allows education degree students to complete their first two years of college at the local community college and transfer in for their final two years.

Since the community college only charges $2,100 a year for in-state students, Holly could graduate paying $27,800 for her degree instead of $47,200 by completing her first two years at the local community college, shaving another $19,400 off of her college costs.

Holly will also check for scholarship and grant opportunities at each of the two schools to get the full financial picture before making a college decision. Since she put off college for two years after high school, she was able to save $25,000 toward her college costs while she worked full-time at a local dental office as a receptionist. The money Holly has saved—along with her plans to work part-time during school—will allow her to pay cash for her degree if she goes with the lowest-priced college option.

By choosing your route to college graduation carefully, and by minimizing what you spend while earning your college degree, you can graduate free of student loan debt and put your postgraduate salary to good use as you save to fund your ERP.

Encouragement for Avoiding Fixed Debt: Focus on Your *Why*

As I've mentioned in previous chapters, focusing on your *why* will help make decisions about how you spend your money much easier. If you find yourself tempted to take out auto or other fixed-debt loans, revisit your list of *why* you want to retire early. Give yourself some extra encouragement for avoiding taking on fixed debt and paying off the fixed debt that you currently have at a faster pace. Saving enough money to retire early is a long journey for most people. Staying on track to accomplish a goal that is a decade or two away takes effort. It can be easy as you watch your net worth grow to think "I'm doing well enough" and start becoming lax on your goals.

Regularly refocusing on your *why* gives you new energy to keep going and not settle for "good enough." You may need to spend some time each month visualizing what life after early retirement will be like in order to stay motivated. Or you may need to make new charts with new pictures from time to time just to keep that psychological momentum going. No matter how far away your goal is, remember why you chose to make early retirement a goal in the first place. Staying focused on that *why* will help get you across the finish line.

CHAPTER 6

Credit Card Debt Can Kill Retirement Plans

Carrying credit card debt has become so common in today's society that most people don't think twice when their cards aren't paid off each month. Instead, it has become normal to buy something as long as you can afford the minimum monthly payment. It wasn't always this way, however. In this section we'll learn about the history of credit card debt and how things have changed, how revolving debt works and how it can shatter your plans to retire early, and how to pay off any credit card debt you may currently have and avoid using credit card debt in the future.

It might surprise you to know that credit card debt and the use of debt in general was not considered acceptable one hundred years ago.

The History of Credit Card Debt

The widespread use of consumer credit and debt is relatively new to people. In the eighteenth and nineteenth centuries, debt was generally issued on a store-by-store basis as a way to purchase things people needed until money came in from their different ventures. For instance, a farmer might ask for credit at the local merchant and then pay that debt in full once harvest time came and he sold his crops. The difference between this type of credit and the credit we use today is that credit was considered a temporary situation at that time. For instance, the farmer might run out of money earned from his harvest in May, and then use credit at the local store until September when the crops were harvested, at which time he would pay his debt in full. Today, things are different and using credit and making payments have become a constant part of life for many people; the cycle of borrowing and paying leads to a permanent state of debt. Additionally, credit in the 1800s and early 1900s was used as a way to purchase needs such as food, whereas today credit is used to purchase both needs and wants.

The first widespread use of what we today call credit cards started with the Diners Club card. This card was first issued in 1950 and served traveling businessmen who needed to pay for meal and entertainment expenses while on the road. Within the first two years, there were 42,000 Diners Club card holders in the United States.

The first all-inclusive credit card was created in 1958 and was called the BankAmericard, which would later become what we now know as Visa. Originally issued only in California, the card expanded for use out of state in 1966. Those first credit cards had to be paid in full at the end of every month, just like any other bill. It was 1987 before the first major credit card allowed consumers to pay a minimum payment on the balance instead of paying the entire balance, although some private store cards allowed minimum payments at that time.

The Case Against Debt

Credit used to be viewed as the risk that it is. Consider what these famous people said about it:

"Rather go to bed without dinner than to rise in debt."
—Benjamin Franklin

"Let every man, every corporation, and especially let every village, town, and city, every country and state, get out of debt and stay out of debt. It is the debtor that is ruined by hard times."
—Rutherford B. Hayes

"Never spend money before you have it."
—Thomas Jefferson

"The one aim of these financiers is world control by the creation of inextinguishable debt."
—Henry Ford

Henry Ford, founder of Ford Motor Company, was staunchly against using debt to finance vehicles. General Motors started allowing consumers to finance cars in 1919, but the Ford Company only allowed customers to purchase cars with cash or via what we know today as a layaway plan, depositing a few dollars each month toward the eventual purchase of a car with cash.

The founder of retail giant JCPenney, James Cash Penney, had the same philosophy. He ran his company without debt and kept thousands of cash in savings, which allowed the company to keep afloat even during the Great Depression.

Clearly things have changed. In 2016 the average credit card balance for those carrying debt month-to-month was more than $16,000.

How Revolving Debt Works

There are two basic different types of debt: revolving and install-ment. An installment loan has a set number of payments, usually a fixed payment amount (except in the case of adjustable rate loans), and is paid in full once you've made all those set payments; at that time the loan gets closed out by the issuer. A car loan is an example of install-ment debt.

Revolving debt involves:

- An available balance (the total amount you can borrow at once), which can increase or decrease over time
- The ability to use some or all of that available balance
- Differentiating payments based on the current month's balance due
- The ability to pay off the balance in full, make minimum pay-ments, or make a payment of any dollar amount as long as it is more than the minimum payment amount requested by the lender
- Credit that becomes available again as the balance is paid down

With fixed debt, the original loan amount never changes; as you pay down the balance, it gets smaller. Revolving debt doesn't work like that. Your balance decreases with payments, but it also increases with new credit purchases. Basically, you borrow the money over and over again—that's where the "revolving" comes in. On top of that, credit card companies created the "minimum payment" scheme that allows you to pay only a small percentage of your total balance due and charges interest (at very high rates) until the full balance is paid (and sometimes even longer). Credit cards and lines of credit are examples of types of revolving credit.

The minimum payment system of providing credit to consumers has made it easier and more tempting for people to live above their means and buy things on credit rather than pay cash. Corporations have taken advantage of the ease in borrowing to extend credit to willing consumers.

Because lenders have made it easier to borrow, consumers have naturally followed suit and borrowed more.

How Credit Card Debt Shatters Your ERP

America has become a nation of borrowers, and with that borrowing mind-set as the norm early retirement has become a far-off dream for those unwilling to do things differently. But you know better. You've defined your goals and are committed to a plan to do what most people aren't willing to do.

Two of the major ways you'll be able to fund your ERP faster is by understanding the dangers behind carrying debt and by learning how to avoid debt as much as possible—especially credit card debt.

Putting something on a credit card is easy and common these days. Most often, credit card debt is a result of living beyond one's means. There are several dangers that come with carrying credit card debt. First, if you're carrying credit card balances over each month it means you've developed a habit of living above your means. As long as this is the case, you'll never have the long-term security of having enough money to retire early and remain financially secure.

Second, credit card debt often comes with high interest rates. As of the third quarter of 2016, the average interest rate that credit card holders paid was 13.76 percent. Paying such a high interest rate on any kind of a loan will seriously deter any plans to grow wealth. If you're carrying the average credit card balance of $16,000, you'll be paying over $2,200 per year (roughly $183 a month) in interest. And those numbers don't include other potential hidden costs, such as rate increases, late payment fees, and additional interest charges that can come from new purchases when you're running a balance. On the other hand, if you were to invest that $183 per month for thirty years at eight percent, you would have over $250,000 in your ERP account.

My take on credit cards is that if you're going to use them, be sure you're using them for purchases that are in line with your budget, and pay the card in full at the end of each month. Never use them for a purchase that hasn't been planned for ahead of time.

How to Avoid Running Up Credit Card Debt

How can you live a life without debt? Doesn't "everyone" have debt? While it's true that carrying debt has become normal in today's society, it is possible—and vital to an ERP—to live without debt. If you're going to reach your early retirement goals, you have to start learning to think differently than most people. Just as early retirement isn't "normal," living a life without credit card debt isn't considered "normal" by the majority of society.

However, living a life without credit card debt is vital to reaching your ERP goals. It's about making a choice. You can choose to live beyond your means now and spend decades paying for it, or you can choose your path to early retirement and avoid living beyond your means by choosing not to accumulate credit card debt.

Following are some suggestions for how to avoid debt.

Avoid Lifestyle Creep

As most people move up in their careers, they feel obligated to make sure their appearance matches their income. They buy bigger houses, drive more expensive cars, wear more expensive clothes, and take fancier vacations. Well-meaning loved ones tell them they "deserve" to spend more. Saving can become more difficult as temptations to spend come their way.

It's up to you to decide whether lifestyle creep is worth giving up your goal of early retirement. As they say in the personal finance world, the freedom that comes with not having money worries is priceless. Are you willing to forgo lifestyle inflation in exchange for financial freedom?

Case Study: Jill and Noah Experience Lifestyle Creep

Jill and Noah married right out of college and quickly caught a case of "lifestyle creep." Their combined $120,000 in gross income made them confident they could "have it all." Five years after they said "I do," they had a sizable mortgage, $20,000 in credit card debt, and $55,000 in auto loan debt. Their monthly payments on that debt were nearly $1,200 ($300 per month as a minimum payment on the credit card, $400 per month on one auto loan, and $500 per month on the other), and what's worse, only a portion of those payments were going toward principal; they were paying $375 a month in interest on the car loans and credit cards.

Money was tight—especially with the $2,500 mortgage payment for their new house. Then Noah and Jill caught the early retirement bug. They sat down and made a plan for paying off their debt quickly. They sold their new cars and bought two inexpensive, quality used cars with the $10,000 in cash they had in savings—money they had saved up before they bought their mini-mansion.

They buckled down, cut unnecessary expenses, and worked hard to pay off the $20,000 in credit card debt that was left after they paid off their car loans. When the debt was paid off eighteen months later, they funneled the $1,200 per month that they were paying for consumer debt—and the $400 per month they saved from cutting expenses—into an ERP. If they contribute $1,600 every month for twenty-one years into their ERP, making no withdrawals and earning 8 percent annual returns, they'll have over $1 million in their investment account (after twenty-one years) and will be able to retire and do something they love instead of being tied to their jobs because of debt payments.

Noah and Jill's story proves that even if you do fall prey to lifestyle creep, you can work your way out and succeed at reaching your goal of retiring early. Keeping your *why* in mind and posting it somewhere you'll see often will help you avoid inflating your lifestyle in the first place, but it will also motivate you to get off the spinning wheel of monthly debt payments and start pushing toward your goal of financial independence.

Commit to Paying Cash for Purchases

Another way to avoid credit card debt is to commit to paying cash for what you buy. If you don't have the cash, you simply don't buy it.

A good way to help ensure you have enough money for what you need when living a cash-only lifestyle is to use the budget you created in Chapter 2. By setting monthly spending amounts in each spending category before you get your paycheck, you can ensure you won't spend cash meant for groceries on tickets to a rock concert that weren't in your budget.

Keep Credit Cards Out of Your Wallet

The more accessible credit cards are, the easier they will be to use for unplanned purchases. By keeping your credit cards in difficult-to-reach places, such as keeping them in a safety deposit box or having someone you trust hold on to them for you, you can minimize the temptation to use them for impulse purchases.

Is a Rewards Card Worth Using?

Many people use a credit card for every purchase in order to earn the rewards that come with using the card. While this can be beneficial, it's also a plan that comes with high risk. If you are committed to using a credit card for the purpose of gaining rewards, consider putting the following safeguards in place.

1. **Track your spending:** By tracking the amount of money you spend each month, you have a safeguard in place that will help ensure you're not going over budgeted amounts even if you are paying them with a credit card.

2. **Pay the balance in full each month:** When using a credit card for rewards purposes, it's vital to pay the card balance in full every month—no questions asked. If you don't, you'll be paying monthly interest on the card that can reduce or negate any rewards you are earning.

3. **Say "no" to impulse purchases:** One of the dangers of using a credit card for rewards is that it becomes very convenient to use the card for impulse purchases. In order to avoid running up debt, it's crucial to have the self-discipline to avoid impulse purchases.

4. **Stick to your budget:** Committing to sticking with your budget is another important safeguard that will help you avoid

accumulating debt if you're using a credit card for rewards. Make sure you are still making and utilizing a written budget every month.

Paying Off Credit Card Debt—A Fantastic Investment

You could look at paying off credit card debt as an investment with a guaranteed high rate of return. As mentioned previously, the average credit card interest rate consumers are paying today is 13.76 percent. When you pay off your credit card debt, your rate of return is equal to the interest percentage you are paying on the card each month. By paying off your credit cards you are beating the average ROI of the stock market and reducing the amount of cash you'll need each month in retirement at the same time.

If you've already accumulated credit card debt and want to pay it off in order to boost your ERP, following are some tips that will help you pay off the debt in a timely manner.

Commit to Stop Using Credit Cards

It's important once you've decided to pay off your credit card debt to commit to no longer using credit cards. Cut them up, freeze them, do whatever you need to do to make credit card use a thing of the past—now and after you've paid your credit card balances in full. Start using a cash-only system as we talked about earlier. You can use the cash envelope system, or use your debit card and make sure you're only spending from the money you have available in your checking account. Again, budgeting is crucial here because it will help you to live within your means.

Cut Expenses and Increase Income

The more money you can find by reducing your expenses, the faster you'll pay off your debt. Consider eliminating most or all unnecessary expenses from your budget for a certain time and put all extra funds toward paying off your credit card debt quickly. Look at your budget and analyze every expense. Be honest with yourself about which current budget expenses are needs and which are wants. Are you paying for cable TV? Do you have magazine or newspaper subscriptions that can be canceled? Are your grocery costs higher than they need to be? Can you reduce your clothing budget or your personal care budget?

You can also come at this from the flipside. Increasing income will also give you more money to put toward credit card payoff and result in your reaching debt freedom faster. Second jobs, overtime hours at work, and side hustles such as babysitting, pet sitting, and mowing lawns are some of the ways you can increase your income.

Avalanche or Snowball?

There are two main methods money experts recommend using to pay off credit card debt: avalanche and snowball. The debt avalanche method of credit card debt payoff involves paying off your credit cards starting with the card that charges the highest rate of interest. Make a list of your credit cards in order of interest rate, starting with the highest charged rate and moving downward. This will tell you which cards to pay off in what order. This is the method that will allow you to save the most money on interest charges.

The snowball method of credit card debt payoff is listing your credit card debts in order of smallest balance to largest. You'll pay the minimum payment on every card, except for the card with the smallest balance. All extra money you find by cutting expenses and increasing income will also go toward the card with the smallest balance.

When the card with the smallest balance is paid off, the money you were paying on that card—and all extra money you find—will then be allocated as extra payments on the next smallest card. You'll continue to snowball the payments on the cards you pay off onto the next targeted card until all of your credit card debt is gone.

While the amount of interest you pay with this method will likely be more than it will with the debt avalanche method, the quick wins you'll get by having paid-in-full debts faster may motivate you more than paying off the highest-rate cards first.

Never Have Late Payments or Missed Payments

Late and missed payments on credit cards can potentially derail your plans to become free of credit card debt. Many credit card companies will not only charge you late fees for missed or late payments, but they'll also increase the interest rate you're paying on your credit card balance. The CARD Act, which was passed in 2009, caps late-fee amounts on occasional late payments at $27 per occurrence. However, credit card companies do have the legal right to increase late-fee amounts for habitual offenders who make late payments more than once in a six-month period. The companies also have the right to raise interest rates on new purchases as long as they give you a forty-five-day notice, and they may also be able to raise interest rates on existing balances if a customer has made one or more late payments.

If you are habitually late on your credit card bill, this can add up to big money out of your pocket. Interest charges and late fees on credit cards are added to your card balance, which means you will have a higher balance and it will take more time for you to pay off the credit card. For your money's sake, it's important to set up auto-payments or put some other type of reminder in place to make sure you don't miss a credit card payment or pay the card later than the due date.

Always Pay More Than the Minimum Due

The overall goal when working to pay off your credit cards quickly is to always pay more than the minimum due. Minimum payments—when combined with interest—ensure you'll be paying off a credit card for years or even decades to come. If you have a credit card balance of $15,000 and are paying an interest rate of 12 percent and a minimum payment of 2 percent of the balance, it will take you close to thirty years to pay off that credit card—and that's only if you stop making purchases with the card.

However, if you pay a monthly payment of 5 percent of the minimum balance, you cut your payoff time down by more than twenty years.

Other Helpful Tips

There are other steps you can add to your plan that will help you become free of credit card debt—and stay that way: establishing a solid savings account for use as an emergency fund; getting credit card counseling if you are having trouble paying off debt on your own; and refocusing on your *why* can help.

Establish an Emergency Fund

An emergency fund is a buffer between you and the accumulation of debt. It will help you avoid using credit cards to pay for those unexpected expenses such as emergency home and car repairs, unexpected medical bills, and job layoffs.

Most financial experts recommend keeping three to six months' worth of expenses in an emergency fund. While you're working to pay down debt though, a more practical interim goal is to put at least $1,000 into your emergency fund. It might seem tough to save up such a large amount of cash, but by avoiding new debt and maximizing your income you can get it done. Make a line item in your budget to add savings to your emergency fund until it's at a level that makes you feel comfortable.

If you're having trouble saving in your emergency fund as you work to pay off debt or reach other financial goals, consider selling items you no longer use or look for more ways to bring in income until you've fully funded your emergency fund.

Consider Credit Counseling

In some cases you may need to consult a credit counseling agency to pay off your debt. If you have a large, unmanageable amount of credit card debt, a credit counseling agency can help you consolidate that debt into one single monthly payment that will help you pay off the debt quickly. However, not all credit counseling agencies are on the up and up. Here are some ways to know whether a credit counseling agency is reputable:

- **Check with state consumer agencies:** Your state's consumer agency or attorney general's office should be able to direct you to honest credit counseling agencies. You can find contact information for your state attorney general on the National Association of Attorneys General website (www.naag.org).
- **Avoid upfront fees:** Any agency that asks for an upfront fee before providing counseling services should be avoided. Reputable agencies may charge a set-up fee or include a fee in the monthly payment they get from you that will go toward paying off your debts. Make sure you know all the fees up front.
- **Beware of overpromises:** Agencies that say that they can wipe your slate clean or make the process of paying off your credit

cards happen quickly may be scam outfits. Anything that sounds too good to be true in the area of credit counseling probably is.

Credit Counseling or Debt Settlement?

Credit counseling and debt settlement are two different things. A credit counseling agency will help you to work with creditors to manage your debt payments in a way that ensures the cards get paid off but does so in a way that is affordable for you.

A debt settlement agency often charges you a fee and then negotiates with credit card companies to receive a smaller sum than what's due as the paid-in-full balance. While both options can hurt your credit, debt settlement agreements are listed as a charge-off with credit bureaus and reveal the amount of money you were supposed to pay back but didn't. Even though a creditor may agree to a debt settlement plan, it's best for your credit rating if you can pay the owed balance in full through a credit counseling agency even if you can't determine a way to pay them back on your own. While credit counseling can be helpful if your debt balances are too high for you to conquer on your own, debt settlement is generally regarded by most finance experts as an option to avoid. The damage to your credit report and the often unsavory business practices of debt settlement companies can do more harm than good to your financial picture.

Refocus on Your *Why*

Although it can be tough to discipline yourself to minimize spending and put all extra funds toward paying down credit card debt, revisiting your *why* will help you keep on track and stay motivated to reach your goals. Making poster boards or other visuals that will remind you why you started your ERP journey in the first place will help you have a constant reminder of how staying focused on debt payoff will reap great rewards in the long run.

Debt in and of itself is amoral, meaning it doesn't have the capability to be good or to be evil. It's what we do with debt that can make it have either a positive or negative effect. Just know that the more saddled down with debt you become, the further away your goal of retiring early gets.

Deciding what is more important to you—saving to fulfill your early retirement plan or having expensive "stuff" that comes with monthly payments—will help you make the choice that will get you to early retirement sooner rather than later.

CHAPTER 7

Investment Vehicles That Will Get You There

As you save money for early retirement, there are three main ways you can grow your wealth as a means of producing income to support you and your family in early retirement. While there are other options for growing wealth, the three we will discuss here are the most widely used by those who have already reached their early retirement goals.

THE RISKS OF SMALL BUSINESS INVESTING

It is worth noting that most small businesses fail, and those that succeed often don't see steady, reliable growth. This makes investing in them less stable than the other two investment alternatives. However, as many of us know, some of the wealthiest people in the world, such as Mark Zuckerberg and Jeff Bezos, are business owners, so there is a lot of potential wealth on the horizon if you do it right.

The Top Three Investment Vehicles People Use to Retire Early

As you work your ERP, you'll need to have one or more investment avenues to grow the wealth that will help you become financially independent. While there are a number of options for doing that, most people who have already achieved early retirement have done so by investing in one or more of these three different ways:

- Stock market investing
- Real estate investing
- Investing in one or more businesses

These three investing options rise above other choices because they offer the best opportunities for growth over the long term and are most likely to (at least eventually) provide steady income streams once you retire.

Retirement Accounts and Your ERP

For the purposes of early retirement, you might want to consider investing both in retirement and nonretirement accounts. Nonretirement accounts should hold a substantial amount of your money because the purpose of early retirement is generally to retire before official retirement age. However, you should also consider investing some of your money into retirement accounts such as these:

- **401(k):** If your employer offers a 401(k) account, consider taking advantage of it. The pretax contributions lower your annual taxable income. Plus, many employers offer matching programs for 401(k) participants, meaning that if you put in $100, your employer will put in $100 to match your contribution—essentially "free" money.

- **Traditional IRAs:** Monies funneled into traditional IRAs reduce your current taxable income; however, postretirement withdrawals get taxed based on your tax rate at the time of withdrawal.
- **Roth IRAs:** Roth IRA contributions do not reduce your current taxable income. However, the earnings can be withdrawn tax-free after retirement age is reached. In other words, tax-free growth equals free money.

Both kinds of IRAs and non-retirement investment accounts can use nearly any combination of investments, with the exception of certain types of collectibles (such as art or wine) which generally aren't allowed in retirement accounts. Depending on the plan your employer offers, 401(k) accounts have much more limited investment choices. Most employers offer a limited number of mutual funds that you can choose to invest your 401(k) monies in. They will offer some low-risk funds, some moderate-risk funds and some high-risk funds, usually from the same fund family (like Vanguard or Fidelity). As an employee-investor, you can only choose to invest your 401(k) monies in a combination of the funds your employer offers. However, IRAs and non-retirement investments allow a much broader range of mutual funds, along with ETFs (exchange-traded funds), individual stocks, individual bonds, and other more exotic investment types (like commodities, for example). Note that while 401(k) accounts and traditional IRAs are great retirement investment options, you won't be able to access the funds in them without paying penalties until you reach age fifty-nine-and-a-half. So if you want to use a tax-advantaged account for some of your ERP funds, use a Roth IRA.

As an early retiree you'll need to be able to access a good portion of your investment savings before age fifty-nine-and-a-half, and you'll want to do so without having to pay penalties. This is why I recommend investing in the stock market (outside of a formal retirement account), in real estate, or in business to fund early retirement living.

Investing in the Stock Market

The stock market as we refer to it today refers primarily to the corporate shares that trade over the New York Stock Exchange (NYSE) and the NASDAQ (National Association of Securities Dealers Automated Quotations). The ups and downs of the stock market are tracked using major benchmark indexes, such as the Dow Jones Industrial Average (DJIA) and the S&P (Standard & Poor's) 500.

The DJIA focuses on the top thirty blue-chip stocks sold on the US stock market. Blue-chip stocks are stock shares in well-known, large companies such as McDonald's, Coca-Cola, IBM, and Disney. The S&P 500 also tracks a portion of the stock market. Whereas the DJIA tracks the performance of the top thirty companies, the S&P 500 tracks the performance of the top five hundred companies.

The Different Types of Stock Market Investing

Let's take a look at the different ways you can invest in the stock market, starting with individual stocks.

When you buy stock in any corporation, you are basically buying a piece of that company. The cost of the individual stock will vary from day to day based on a combination of overall market performance and the company's individual performance (as well as other things), and price swings can be extremely volatile. Buying individual stocks can be quite risky because the value of your investment is based heavily on one company's performance, and even blue-chip corporations can post losses that send share prices plummeting.

A less risky way to own stock is through mutual funds. A mutual fund is a basket of shares from a variety of different companies. Mutual funds are set up by fund managers, with specific investing strategies in mind; the investment strategy dictates which stocks the fund will hold. Shares in mutual funds are bought (and sold) directly from (and to) the mutual fund company that issued them. There are dozens of different types of mutual funds, but these are the main categories (including some that are not stock-related):

- **Money market funds:** Though these are not stock funds, they are commonly offered by mutual fund families. You won't get a high return on a money market fund, but you will have the security of knowing that your investment is safe. Since money market funds invest primarily in ultra-safe Treasury bills and other short-term debt instruments, they rarely lose principal. This can be a great place to park your emergency fund.

- **Bond funds:** Again, these funds don't hold stocks, but that can be a stabilizing addition to your ERP portfolio. Bond funds, which can hold corporate or government bonds, are designed to provide current income on a steady basis. These funds traditionally aren't as risky as stock funds (unless you invest in a high-risk corporate "junk bond" portfolio), but hold more risk than money market funds. They also typically provide lower returns than stock funds and higher returns than money market funds. As you get older, you may consider investing in a mix of bond and stock mutual funds to reduce your exposure to risk.

- **Equity funds:** These funds are made up primarily of different company stocks. Depending on the specific fund, they can hold small-cap, mid-cap, and large-cap companies; they can invest in US or international markets, specific market sectors (like consumer goods), or even specific industries (like food).
- **Index funds:** Index funds track market indexes, such as the S&P 500 and the DJIA (and there are hundreds more). Because these funds hold the exact same stocks as the index they're tracking, they don't require constant monitoring by a fund manager. This "passive management" maintenance results in lower fund fees for investors, which helps boost your actual returns.
- **ETFs:** Exchange-traded funds (ETF) are similar to mutual funds (in that they hold baskets of different stocks), with one huge difference. ETFs are traded like stocks, over exchanges, rather than directly with the mutual fund company.

WHAT'S A CAP?

A corporation's "market capitalization" (or market cap) is calculated by multiplying the number of outstanding shares by the current share price. Companies with market cap under $2 billion are considered small cap; between $2 billion and $10 billion are mid cap; and $10 billion and bigger are large cap.

The Risks of Investing in the Stock Market

The performance of the stock market is based on many things, including: consumer confidence, the current economy, world events, and the performance of individual companies. Because the market can be volatile, investors can lose large amounts of cash when investing in the stock market. In fact, it's possible to lose your entire investment. However, over the long term the market has always recovered, even from significant crashes.

When the Great Depression struck in 1929, the US suffered a major stock market crash, causing more than $30 billion in losses in a two-day period. The economic collapse that followed caused unprecedented unemployment and foreclosure rates as consumer confidence continued to tumble and spending came to a virtual halt.

In 2008 when the housing bubble burst, it caused a similar reaction in the stock market. That crash, now referred to as the Great Recession, resulted in the loss of $11 trillion from stock portfolios.

Although scenarios such as the Great Depression and Great Recession do happen, they are rare, and, as noted earlier, the long-term ROI of the S&P 500 still stands at 9.7 percent. The long-term history of profitability makes the stock market a solid investment choice for your ERP.

The Stock Market Makes Its Case

Do you remember the story of Ronald Read from Chapter 3? Read made more than $8 million investing in the stock market, all while working jobs such as gas station attendant and janitor. Read made his fortune by investing consistently in blue-chip stocks from well-known companies with a long history of success. That's it. No fancy advisers or college degrees. Just common sense, the willingness to learn, and the power of patience as his wealth grew.

Early retirement and financial independence aren't achievable goals meant only for the wealthy; they're possible for the Ronald Reads of the world as well. You just have to educate yourself. In Appendix B at the back of this book you'll find a glossary of some terms that might be helpful for you to know as you work to determine how stock market investing can help you fund your early retirement.

Stock Market Returns

Now let's talk about stock market returns.

Take a look at the following chart reflecting the performance history of the different sectors of the US stock market over more than eighty years. Of course, past performance is not a guarantee of future performance, but it gives you a pretty good idea of how the stock market rides the economic roller coaster over time.

Market Returns by Decade					
ASSET CLASS	1930S	1940S	1950S	1960S	1970S
S&P 500 Index	−.1	9.2	19.4	7.8	5.9
Large-Cap Value	−5.7	12.7	18.4	9.4	12.9
Small Cap	2.3	14.9	19.2	13.0	9.2
Small-Cap Value	−2.6	19.8	19.6	14.4	14.4

ASSET CLASS	1980S	1990S	2000S	AVERAGE
S&P 500 Index	17.5	18.2	−.9	9.7
Large-Cap Value	20.6	16.8	4.1	11.2
Small Cap	16.8	15.5	9.0	12.7
Small-Cap Value	20.1	16.2	12.8	14.4

(Source: www.marketwatch.com/story/8-lessons-from-80-years-of-market-history-2014-11-19)

Although certain decades (notably the 1930s) resulted in lower returns than others, the long-term returns of the stock market are solid.

Here is a brief overview of each asset class:

- **S&P 500:** This is a collection, selected by economists, of five hundred of the largest and most prominent companies in America that trade on the New York Stock Exchange or NASDAQ.
- **Large-cap value:** These are well-established companies that are worth more than $5 billion and that are trading below their true market value.
- **Small cap:** These companies have a market capitalization between $300 million and $2 billion, giving them plenty of room for growth.
- **Small-cap value:** These are small-cap companies that are trading under their current market value.

As you probably already know, there are many more asset classes than just these, and not all have been as successful. The point is to show that high returns are possible on your investments if you pick the right stocks. However, there are always risks involved.

A Word about Fees

As you manage your investment accounts, it's important to keep in mind that you should track the fees you are paying as well. Most people don't think of fees as being a major roadblock to growing wealth, but they can have a bigger impact on your bottom line than you think.

When you invest in a mutual or other fund there are several types of fees that can be charged:

- **Expense ratio:** The expense ratio defines the percentage of your money that a fund charges each year for operating, management, and administrative expenses. It's important to ask about a fund's expense ratio before you invest in it; you can find that information spelled out in the fund's prospectus. An expense ratio of

1 percent or less is considered reasonable by financial experts (though certain types of actively managed specialty funds may reasonably charge more).

- **Load fees:** Load fees are costs incurred when you buy or sell shares in a fund. A front-end load fee charges you money when you buy the shares, and a back-end load fee charges you money when you sell shares (though these may be waived if you hold the fund for a minimum period before selling). Load fees generally run 3–6 percent. A no-load fund doesn't charge any fees when you buy or sell shares in the fund.

Asking about these types of expenses before you invest in a fund will help you understand exactly what you will be paying for participating in the fund. Fee amounts are an important consideration because although 1, 3, and 5 percent don't seem like big numbers, they can add up to hundreds of thousands of dollars in postretirement monies over the long run. Also, each dollar in fees that you pay means not only one less dollar for you to spend postretirement, but one less dollar for you to earn interest on.

Understanding How Fees Can Impact Your Investments

Another point to consider when you're deciding whether to hire a financial adviser is the impact of adviser fees on your investment returns. Even a very small fee can have a big impact on your investments.

Over a long time portfolio values can suffer largely as a result of fees, so it's important to make your decisions carefully when it comes to financial advisers. The smaller a client's investment portfolio, the bigger impact fees can have. And, remember, you have to pay the adviser's fees even if your investments lose money.

Your Age and Investment Risk

Stocks and equities are generally considered higher risk but have a greater potential for return, and bonds are generally considered lower risk but offer a lower rate of return. The younger you are the more risk you should consider adding to your investment portfolio because the chance for growth (and recovery from losses) is greater.

A general rule of thumb as far as risk and asset allocation is that the percentage of bonds you include in your portfolio should be equal to your age. In other words, if you're thirty, you might want to consider a portfolio that has 30 percent in bonds and 70 percent in stocks or other equities. If you're forty-five, you might want to have a portfolio that consists of 45 percent in bonds and 55 percent in stocks or other equities.

Lowering your risk as you get older allows for a greater chance of growth when you're younger, but improves stability and minimizes potential losses as you get older, so that your investment account becomes less volatile as you get closer to your target retirement age. Maximizing growth potential in your investment account is vital when you are younger, as is seeking stability in your investment account as you grow older.

Smart Tips for Living Off Your Investment Account

Once you've reached that place of financial independence when your ERP is fully funded and ready to go, you'll want to make sure to live smart when it comes to investment account withdrawals. Here are a couple of ways to help ensure your money lasts for the long haul.

The Multiply by Twenty-Five Rule is a popular early retirement rule. If you have twenty-five times your annual expenses in your investment portfolio, that money should last you a lifetime. For instance, if you have $10,000 a year in annual expenses, you need $250,000 in liquid assets that you can withdraw from. If you have $30,000 a year in annual expenses, you should have $750,000 in liquid investment assets that you can withdraw from.

Many financial experts use the 4 percent rule: you should be in a position to withdraw no more than 4 percent from your investment account per year after you retire. On the other hand, other experts say that the 4 percent rule isn't sustainable in this day and age. They cite falling interest rates, longer life spans, and potential variations in investment allocation. The 4 percent rule is based on the idea that your investment account will earn 4 percent every year once you're in retirement. If this projection seems like it might leave you a little short on funds for long-term retirement plans, you can always play it safe and determine the fully funded amount of your ERP based on what is deemed a safe withdrawal rate, or SWR, at 3 or 3.5 percent.

After you've retired, it's important to stick with the postretirement spending plan you calculated. Be careful not to get lax with your budgeting and start spending more than you had planned for. A good goal would be to work to live on 5–10 percent less than you'd planned for in your ERP and bank the savings for unexpected expenses.

Real Estate Investing

There are three main avenues when it comes to investing in real estate, and each has its own set of pros and cons. The first is traditional real estate investing, where you own rental properties and either manage them yourself or work with a management company to maintain the properties and their tenants. The second way is through investing in a real estate investment trust (REIT). The third avenue is crowdfunded real estate.

Pros of Traditional Real Estate Investing

Investing in real estate that you own can have several benefits. First, you have a tangible asset you can control. In other words, traditional real estate investing means you have brick-and-mortar properties in your name (or the name of your business) that you can visit and check on to make sure everything is going well.

Another great thing about owning investment properties is that potential for residual income is high. As long as you are charging a rent that exceeds the total monthly cash expenses for the property, you've got residual income (though you may still have a paper loss for tax purposes due to depreciation expense, further increasing your cash flow). As a bonus, your tenants essentially pay down the mortgage (if you needed one to finance the property), and as the mortgage is paid off your potential for residual income increases.

The possibility of passive income also exists in traditional real estate investing if you hire a property management company to deal with property maintenance and tenant issues. In most cases you'll find that the property value appreciates over time, which will result in a higher net worth for you if you pay down the mortgage in a timely manner.

Case Study: Jacob and Samantha Invest in Real Estate

Jacob and Samantha are in their mid-thirties, and they are in the process of building a real estate portfolio for their ERP. Jacob is a science teacher and Samantha is an administrative assistant for an insurance company. Their combined income is $110,000 per year. For the past five years they've been saving $25,000 per year toward their dream of living off of real estate investments. They know they want about $4,000 a month to live on, so they are working on structuring their real estate portfolio in a way that will accommodate that amount of income.

The first property they buy is a single-family, three-bedroom, two-bath home. The home is in a fairly decent area in their larger metropolitan city. The house was a foreclosure, and they were able to purchase it for roughly $45,000 due to its extensive need of cosmetic repairs and their willingness to pay cash. (Note that this house was in a less expensive area of a major metropolitan city; opportunities like this might not be available depending on where you live.) Jacob and Samantha put $15,000 worth of repairs into the house, so their total cost invested, including closing costs of $3,000, is approximately $63,000.

Jacob and Samantha have been living frugally the past several years and were able to put $125,000 ($25,000 a year for five years) into their "dream" account, so they had plenty of cash to pay for the house. Based on market data, the house will rent for between $1,000 and $1,200 a month. Including landlord expenses such as property taxes, insurance, vacancy rate (a small monthly savings deposit to cover the mortgage payment during any potential vacancies), and maintenance and repairs, they should have expenses ranging roughly in the area of $350 a month. If they can rent the property for $1,000, Jacob and Samantha have just given themselves a $650 per month income, before income taxes.

The following year, Jacob and Samantha decide to purchase another rental property. This time they settle on a triplex that is listed for $160,000. They don't have the cash to pay for the triplex outright, so they put 20 percent down plus closing costs (taken from their savings account) and end up with a mortgage of $1,300 per month, including property taxes and insurance, over a fifteen-year term. They spend

$20,000 in improvements for the property, which needed cosmetic work and a new roof.

This rental property is in a better area of town than the first one they bought, so the main unit rents for more money. Rental unit number 1 is a three-bedroom, two-bath unit that takes up the whole main floor and rents for $1,600 a month. Rental units 2 and 3 are split equally on the upper level and they are each one-bedroom, one-bath units. Each unit rents for $900 a month.

Their costs for landlord expenses for this house run roughly $600 per month (more than the first property since this is a triplex with larger square footage instead of a single-family home), bringing their total outgoing cost to $1,900 per month. Since their incoming rental payments are $3,400 per month, they will have $1,500 per month positive cash flow from this property before income taxes. That cash surplus will increase to nearly $2,800 per month once the fifteen-year mortgage is paid off.

Jacob and Samantha's monthly income from their rental properties is now $2,150 per month.

If they can purchase two more properties that are similar in nature to the first two they bought, they will have reached the monthly income threshold needed for them to quit their full-time jobs and completely live off of their real-estate investing income.

Cons of Traditional Real Estate Investing

Like any investment avenue, there are also negative sides to owning and managing rental properties.

First, there is the time and money it takes to maintain the property and upgrade it as necessary. You'll have to make repairs as things get older and as tenants cause wear and tear on the property. Although you can hire a management company to handle this, doing so will cut into your monthly profit.

The vacancy potential is another con to keep in mind. Depending on how long the house or apartment is vacant after a tenant leaves, the property could have a serious effect on your net worth and annual profit.

Liability issues can be another downside of owning rental properties. You'll need to have the right kind of coverage to provide insurance for potential losses associated with the property, from weather-related issues (like hurricane damage) to personal injury issues (a tenant falls down the stairs, for example).

Also, there is always the risk with real estate rentals that tenants won't pay their rent and you'll have to start eviction proceedings. Sometimes evicting a tenant for nonpayment of rent can be easy; other times it can involve court time and lawsuits. Knowing the laws in the state where you own your rental properties can help you handle nonpayment by tenants more efficiently.

Buying rental properties by yourself also comes with a higher upfront capital than crowdfunded real estate or REIT investing. Most lenders generally require at least 20 percent down on a rental property purchase, on top of closing costs.

One final con of traditional real estate investing is that your investment isn't liquid as it is when you own stocks in the stock market. If you need to cash out the investment, you'll have to wait until the property sells and closes before you can get the cash you need.

Case Study: Bryan and Hannah Invest in Traditional Real Estate

Bryan and Hannah decided that they wanted to fund their ERP via traditional real estate investing. After doing some research, they chose to look for a rental property in a modestly priced neighborhood not too far from their home.

After months of looking, they found a three-bedroom, two-bath home in Atlanta, which was in good shape but needed some cosmetic work. The purchase price for the home was $120,000. I should add here that when investing in real estate, you are not looking to purchase an average home. Instead, you are searching for a stellar deal. Foreclosures, homes that people need to sell quickly, and homes that have solid frames but are in need of extensive cosmetic work are ideal, as you will be able to purchase them for much lower than the average-priced home.

With 20 percent down they'll need a mortgage of $96,000. Since interest rates for investment properties are usually higher than interest rates for owner-occupied properties, the thirty-year mortgage for their rental will come with a 5.25 percent interest rate.

Their total mortgage payment (including property taxes and insurance) will be roughly $730 per month. However, they've decided to bank another $170 per month to cover potential repairs and vacancy costs. This means that their total outlay for the property each month will be around $900. Since rental properties of similar size in that area rent for approximately $1,200–$1,300 per month, Bryan and Hannah are counting on an income of at least $300 a month from that property.

If they are able to pay off the home in ten years by paying $500 extra on the mortgage each month, their income will then jump to at least $1,000 per month.

By purchasing a few more rental properties of similar value, they can establish a good base for their postretirement income using traditional real estate investing.

Some might wonder why I recommend using extra money to pay off the mortgage faster instead of investing that money for a potentially higher rate of return. Let's say that instead of using any extra money to pay off the mortgage, Bryan and Hannah invested it instead. Let's use a figure of $500 for simplicity's sake, and say they invested that each month at 8 percent. At the end of ten years they'd have $93,872. Multiplying that by a 4 percent dividend rate you'd have $312.90 per month in income. However, you'd still have the mortgage payment. Whereas financially it may be better to invest and earn the higher rate, paying off the mortgage faster would give them increased income faster. The other factor is that 8 percent isn't a guaranteed return; the market could crash, etc. By paying off the mortgage they'd earn a solid guaranteed 5.25 percent return and have more monthly income earlier.

Real Estate Investment Trusts

A real estate investment trust, or REIT, is similar to a mutual fund, but it holds mortgages, income-producing real estate, or real estate development companies instead of shares in company stocks. Many REITs are traded on the NYSE, but there are also private REITs and unlisted public REITs.

Like crowdfunded real estate, which I talk about next, REITs can be beneficial for investors as they involve little work on the part of the investor. There's no property management or dealing with tenants. Returns on REIT will vary depending on the real estate market. I'm not necessarily for or against investing in REITs; however, I do recommend—as with any other investment—that you do your research thoroughly before investing in them.

Crowdfunded Real Estate Investing

The last option for investing in real estate is referred to as crowdfunded real estate investing. Investing with crowdfunding means you are teaming up with other investors to finance the real estate ventures.

When you invest in real estate in this manner, you put up cash that goes toward helping others purchase rental properties (usually commercial in nature or multifamily housing units), which they will own and manage. In return for your cash investment you are entitled to part of the profits the property produces.

Pros of Crowdfunded Real Estate Investing

When you invest in real estate via crowdfunding, you don't have to deal with the purchase, management, or maintenance of the property. It's largely a hands-off venture, save for monitoring the account.

Another upside to investing in real estate this way is that you can start with less up-front capital. Depending on the crowdfunding company you choose, you can start investing with $1,000–$5,000, as opposed to the 20 percent or more you'll need to put down if you purchase a real estate property on your own.

Crowdfunded real estate investing may also boast higher returns, as experienced real estate investors (who are proficient at spotting good deals) choose the properties, often lucrative commercial real estate.

Cons of Crowdfunded Real Estate Investing

Crowdfunding in real estate has its cons as well as its pros. The first potential con is that crowdfunded investing is not liquid. Unlike investing in REITs or in the stock market, when you participate in crowdfunded real estate investing you're often locked into an investment period, just as if you purchased a CD (certificate of deposit). You could be out some cash due to penalties if you withdraw the money before the period expires.

Some crowdfunding companies allow only accredited investors to participate. If you don't have an income of at least $200,000 per year ($300,000 for married couples) or a minimum $1 million net worth (the requirements for accredited investors), you may be denied the opportunity to invest in specific crowdfunded real estate projects.

A third con to investing in real estate in this manner is that you have no control over the asset. You're simply a shareholder, hoping the investment does well.

Finally, most real estate crowdfunding companies do charge small (typically 1 percent) asset management fees, which reduce your share of earnings.

Case Study: Chloe and Jayden Invest in Crowdfunded Real Estate

Chloe and Jayden have decided to help fund their ERP via crowdfunded real estate investing. They're not accredited investors, but they've found a crowdfunding company that allows investors that aren't accredited to participate.

After researching scores of investment opportunities on the crowdfunding website, Jayden and Chloe have chosen to invest $10,000 in a real estate venture that will be used to purchase a large apartment complex.

They've chosen an investor who has a long-term history in real estate investing and has successfully bought and managed several other rental acquisitions. The investment has historically netted 10 percent returns annually and they eventually decide to keep investing in this fund after their initial $10,000 investment, adding an additional $20,000 per year to the fund for fifteen years. At that point their investment would be worth roughly $677,222. If the yield was still 10 percent at that time, they would be earning nearly $68,000 per year from this investment.

Residential Real Estate Investing versus Commercial Real Estate Investing

If you've chosen to go with traditional real estate investing instead of crowdfunded real estate investing, you'll need to decide whether to invest in residential real estate properties or commercial real estate properties. It's good to know some of the facts about each type of investing before making a decision. Both have their pros and cons.

Pros of Investing in Residential Real Estate

Investing in residential properties usually requires a smaller down payment than a commercial property. Most lenders require no more than 20 percent down when purchasing a residential investment property. This could be good for your ERP if your liquid cash is limited or if you don't want to tap into too much of your cash.

Banks and lenders also usually allow up to a thirty-year mortgage term for a residential rental property. Although I don't suggest taking on a thirty-year loan, the flexibility here will help you with cash flow (a longer loan term offers smaller monthly payments) and give you a longer time to pay off the loan. Remember, the longer your loan term, the more interest you'll end up paying over the life of the loan.

Cons of Investing in Residential Real Estate

Depending on what type of residential property you purchase, a vacancy period can have a big impact on your ERP. If you own a single-family rental property and that property goes vacant, all of your investment income is gone until you find a new tenant.

Multifamily rental properties can help ease the burden of potential vacancy rates but they also require a higher purchase price and, therefore, a higher down payment to buy the property.

Also, purchasing residential investments as opposed to commercial investments will likely result in a smaller monthly profit. Commercial properties tend to have longer-term tenants (businesses typically don't move as often as families), and offer room to charge higher rents.

Pros of Investing in Commercial Real Estate

With commercial real estate investing there are good sides and not-so-good sides as well.

Commercial real estate properties generally charge higher rental rates and often have more spaces to rent out. This can result in higher profits for the investor. Because a commercial real estate building will often have more space to rent, potential vacancies have less of an impact on the investor's profit than does a vacancy in a residential rental.

Cons of Investing in Commercial Real Estate

Because commercial properties cost more and may present a higher risk to lenders, banks often require a larger down payment for a commercial property purchase. It's not uncommon for lenders to ask for 25–35 percent down for commercial real estate purchases.

Another factor to consider when contemplating a commercial real estate investment is the term of the loan. Although banks calculate the monthly mortgage payment for a commercial property based on a twenty- or thirty-year loan amortization, those commercial loans often come with a balloon payment, meaning the loan must be paid in full or refinanced in five years. This could put you in a bind if your financial situation changes for the worse over the five-year period before the loan comes due.

Real Estate Investing and the Risks

In spite of all of the benefits of real estate investing, it does come with some risks. One big risk is the possibility of a housing crash, as happened in the Great Recession of 2008 and during the Great Depression. Substantial housing value crashes may be rare but they do happen.

Another risk is the amount of debt taken on to purchase your properties. There are many inventive ways to invest directly in real estate with little money down; however, the less money you put down on your rental properties, the larger the risk of losing the property to foreclosure or being upside down on the property (meaning the remaining mortgage balance is more than the fair market value of the property) during tough financial times. So although it is possible to invest in real estate with a minimal amount of cash down, there are some guidelines to use when buying real estate that will put a buffer between you and potential asset depreciation.

Real Estate Returns

If you look at real estate investing simply from the viewpoint of asset appreciation, you'll find that historically it doesn't perform all that well. One study comments:

> "From 1928 to 2012 the Case-Shiller Home Price Index returned 3.71% per year. So it just barely beats the long-term rate of inflation (about 3.35% per year). Stocks returned 9.31% a year and bonds had an annual return of 5.10%."

That 3.71 percent is a measure of the average sales prices of single-family homes, based on arms' length sales (meaning people buying and selling houses to live in), so it's not strictly comparable to investment returns. However, if you were to look at the performance of REITs (real estate investment trusts, which offer individual investors a way to participate in the lucrative commercial and residential rental real estate markets), you would see a different story. From the end of 1978 through March 31, 2016, the total returns for exchange-traded US Equity REITs have averaged 12.87 percent per year. As you can see, REITs can perform better than the overall stock market, despite the recession and housing crisis.

When looking at residential real estate from strictly an appreciation standpoint it may not look like much of an investment. However, one important factor is missing from this equation: the income that can be earned by renting out the property. Although the individual rental properties an investor owns might not appreciate as much as the stock market, they can produce a consistent monthly income. This is why financially independent people choose over and over again to invest in real estate rentals.

Smarter Real Estate Investing

Here are some guidelines that will help you minimize risk and maximize profit.

The first rule in smarter real estate investing is to put down a substantial down payment. Twenty percent down for residential and 25 percent down for commercial is what most lenders require and is the minimum I recommend putting down.

The second rule: get the shortest-term mortgage you can swing. Although you'll have a much smaller monthly payment by getting a thirty-year mortgage on your rental properties, using a fifteen-year mortgage instead will save you tens of thousands of dollars in interest payments over the life of the loan and increase your equity in the property at a faster rate.

Some real estate investors argue that it's best to take out a thirty-year mortgage on investment properties and invest the difference in higher-producing investment assets, keeping the mortgage as long as you can.

They say that using "cheap debt" in order to make more money in the long run is a smart strategy for increasing wealth. While that may be a great idea in general, the fact is that we live in a world that can produce recessions and depressions, all of which can hinder your financial state. Also, the faster you pay off your investment property, the less you'll pay in interest and the faster your monthly cash flow will increase.

Speaking of cash flow, another tenet of successful real estate investing is to purchase a property from which "cash flows" from the outset. A property provides cash flow when the monthly rental rate minus the monthly expenses to pay the mortgage and maintain the property results in a positive number. For instance, if the rental rate on your property is $1,200 per month and the expenses per month are $1,100, then the property cash flows by $100 per month.

It's important when calculating cash flow that you include an extra monthly dollar amount that can be put into savings to cover any future repairs or periods of vacancy. This extra savings will help ensure your property isn't producing cash one month and leaving you in the negative the next. When evaluating a potential property purchase, an ideal cash flow amount is 5–10 percent of what the monthly cost for the house is including savings for repairs and vacancy rates. For example, if the total monthly cost of the property is $1,000, a good cash flow would be $50–$100 per month, making the rental rate at least $1,050 –$1,100 per month.

Some people buy investment properties with no cash flow, basing their potential ROI (return on investment) on property appreciation. A smart investor, however, purchases on the basis of cash flow and not solely on potential future appreciation. Appreciation of a property won't help you fund your ERP for years, but a steady cash flow will.

Market cycles can also impact how well your real estate investments perform. Before purchasing an investment property, it's important to be aware of how the housing market is performing. For example, those who bought houses in 2005 and 2006, right before the housing bubble burst, lost between 20 and 30 percent of their real estate wealth almost overnight. Knowing the current state of the housing market before you invest will help you to make smarter property purchases. There are four phases of the real estate cycle: expansion, peak, contraction, and trough.

- The **expansion** cycle is when the economy is growing. Expansion cycles can last a long time if the economy is well managed.
- The **peak** cycle occurs when the expansion cycle morphs into a contraction cycle. It's when housing prices are at their highest and the economy is starting to get volatile, as occurred in 2006.
- The **contraction** cycle starts at the peak and ends at the trough. Signs of a contraction cycle are a weakening economy. Stock market rates may be declining. Unemployment rates may be increasing.
- The **trough** cycle runs between the contraction and the expansion cycles. This is when real estate prices are at their lowest. It's when the economy hits bottom, as we saw in 2008.

For example, when the recession happened in 2008 there was a contraction in the market and home values dropped. Then shortly after you saw a trough where prices began to stabilize. Then after that prices begin to rise until they hit their peak and at some point a contraction occurs once again. Right now we're in an expansion market. Prices are going up and there is more demand than supply. Eventually prices will top out and the cycle will start over.

Investing with OPM

Some real estate investing experts encourage the use of other people's money (OPM) to finance real estate investing ventures. They propose minimizing the use of your own cash for the investment and getting outside investors to contribute the cash needed for a down payment on the property and giving those investors a percentage of the monthly profit on the deal. This is basically crowdfunded investing from the other side: you are the real estate expert who makes the deals, and investors contribute to your purchases in exchange for a piece of the monthly income.

Although investing in real estate with OPM can have good results, it's important to understand all the risks involved. Real estate investing—like any investing venture—comes with risks. When you're risking your own money that's one thing, but risking (and potentially losing) someone else's money is a whole other ball game. It can not only cost you money, it can cost you relationships as well.

Using OPM to invest is especially dangerous to those with a low risk tolerance. If you choose to purchase real estate using other people's money, be sure that both you and your fellow investors are well aware of the risks, and make a plan to pay back the money as soon as possible.

How much cash you have to invest, your risk tolerance level, and your real estate investing knowledge will all be factors in whether you choose to invest in residential real estate or commercial real estate—or whether you choose to invest in real estate at all.

It's important to do your research thoroughly to determine which type of real estate investing is best for you, but in the end you might find that other types of investments are a better choice for you.

Are Tax-Forfeited Properties a Scam?

Real estate infomercial experts claim that investors can make big money by purchasing tax-forfeited properties. Here's how the purchase of such a property really works.

First, the homeowner must be delinquent on his or her property taxes. The laws governing delinquent property seizure vary from state to state. Some states can seize properties after only a few months in delinquency; others have to wait a year or longer before they can seize the property.

After the property is seized, the government entity auctions it off. Some local governments hold the auctions at the county courthouse, while others hold online auctions. Tax-forfeited property auctions are generally run by the local sheriff's department.

Although buyers can sometimes get bargain prices on tax-forfeited homes, there are also many drawbacks to buying homes in this manner. If you're thinking about investing in real estate via tax-forfeited properties, there are some key factors to consider.

Many times tax-forfeited properties are in rough shape due to their previous owners having financial or other problems. Not all counties allow potential buyers to inspect the house prior to auction, and it can be extra risky to purchase a tax-forfeited property sight unseen.

Even after you win the auction for the property and hand the county a check, you may not own the house free and clear. Many times there are additional liens on the property from banks or contractors. Before offering to purchase a tax-forfeited property, find out if there are any existing liens on it. This information can usually be found in the county court records.

Every county runs tax-forfeited property auctions a bit differently. Some might ask the bid winner to put a large down payment on the property at the time of auction and pay the rest within a certain period. Other counties might require a cashier's check for the full price at the time of auction. Be sure you know what the county's rules are regarding payment for bid winners of tax-forfeited properties and be financially prepared to comply at the time of auction.

With tax-forfeited properties, owners are often still living in the house. Other times, the owners have left but squatters have taken up residence on the property. Know the current situation regarding who is living in the house and what the local rules are for evicting current tenants before bidding on a tax-forfeited property. Local laws don't always make evicting existing tenants easy, even if those tenants have no legal right to be there.

Buying tax-forfeited properties can be a good way to gain wealth through real estate—however, it's not as easy as TV infomercials make it seem. There can be a lot of expenses and a lot of competition, and you need to know the exact rules of the county in which the home is located before putting a bid on a property. In other words, proceed with caution. Study and become an expert on tax-forfeited properties before you buy.

Business Ownership

There are a couple of different ways you can invest in a business as a means to fund your ERP. The first is by buying into an existing business to help it expand. The second is by starting your own business.

Investing in an existing business can take a lot of the work out of the picture. Since the business is already up and running, you as the investor have solid numbers to view that show historical performance and costs.

If you start your own business from the ground up, all potential numbers are based on projections. However, starting your own business means that you are largely in control of every aspect of helping the business grow. The following information will give you more to think about as you decide whether investing in an existing business or starting your own business is best for you.

Buying Into Existing Non-Franchise Businesses

If you buy into an existing non-franchise business as an inactive or silent partner, you'll likely have very little work to do other than to hand over a check and hope that the business grows.

If you buy in as an active business partner, you'll do your part to help run and grow the business. If you decide to work to fund your ERP by buying into an existing business, there are things you can do to ensure you're making a wise choice in the business you're choosing to invest in.

If you are buying in as joint owner, make sure the existing business owner is clear about whether you are to be an active partner or a passive partner. If you are taking over and buying as full owner, ask the current owner why he or she wants to sell. Buying in as a partner means you will be working with existing management to increase business. However, taking over a business from an existing owner means you're likely on your own after ownership changes hands. If the current owner bows out of the business completely after the sale, you've got very little recourse once the deal is made. Therefore, it's important to get a clear picture of how the business is running currently before you agree to buy. To do that, consider asking these questions:

- *Can you show me the company's financials?* The business owner should have a complete set of audited financial statements (a balance sheet, a statement of profit and loss, and a statement of cash flows) covering the past several years. She should also have copies of tax returns available. Other information to collect includes customer lists (including the amounts they currently owe the business), vendor lists, and a key personnel roster. When you're buying into a business, it's reasonable to ask for the current owner's personal financial statements and tax returns as well.

- *What will you do with the money I invest?* Ask the owner for a detailed business plan spelling out how your money will be used. The plan should make good financial sense. For example, it might make sense to invest if management is looking to expand, either in locations or product lines. It would not make sense to invest if the business is already struggling or if the owner is strapped for cash.
- *What have been the company's greatest challenges, and how have you overcome them?* A business owner should know what obstacles the company has faced and should be able to share the action plan that helped her overcome those challenges.
- *What will my role as part owner be? What is your current role?*
- *Do you have any current, previous, or potential lawsuits?*
- *Does one customer produce the majority of your business or are sales spread out more evenly?*
- *What additional skills are needed in order to run this business more effectively and efficiently?*
- *Do you have any slow seasons during the year?*
- *Who are your suppliers and what is your relationship with them?*

By getting a clear picture of the buy-in amount and of what's expected of you as the new joint business owner, you can make an informed decision about buying into an existing business.

Let's look at the following case study as an example of the right way to go into business.

Case Study: Derek and Olivia Start a Business

Derek and Olivia decide that the best way for them to grow the wealth needed to retire early is to build a business that someone else can eventually run for them. Since Derek and Olivia have good management skills, they decide to open a cleaning business that focuses on cleaning commercial buildings. They spend the first five years of the business gaining clients and hiring a quality team to do the work of cleaning the buildings. Eventually, they franchise out the company and after ten years their focus is on occasional meetings with potential franchise owners. They have hired qualified employees to conduct most meetings and to train new franchise owners. They now have 25 franchise branches in the United States, and their personal income from the business equals $12,000 a month before taxes. Meeting with potential franchise owners takes them less than five hours per week, and they have plenty of time to live as they want to live.

Derek and Olivia weren't comfortable using stock market or real estate investing as options to grow wealth, but they knew that they were good at cleaning and good at managing people, so they used the skills they had to build a thriving business that would eventually allow them to retire early.

Buying a Business Outright

If you have a good business sense and enough capital for a deal that works in your favor, consider buying the entire business instead of buying into it. Buying the business outright makes you the main decision-maker, so you don't have to worry about partners. Two very important numbers you'll want to know when buying a business are its annual net profit and net cash flow (for at least the past five years). Many people seek to value a business based on its gross revenues. However, this is not a good way to go. For example, a company could be bringing in $100,000 per year in revenues but have profits of only $15,000 per year—that might not be a great investment. Because you are looking for something to help you retire early, you need a proven profitable business with strong cash flow.

Keep in mind, there are many factors that go into valuing a company. One measure involves a multiple of the net profit. It's common to value a company by multiplying its annual net profit by four. So if it is doing $15,000 per year, you could offer $60,000 for that business. The multiple can vary per industry, so check with your accountant to make sure you are getting the best deal. You'll also want your accountant to perform a detailed analysis of the company's financial statements and tax returns, have an appraiser value the company's assets (which may include top customers), and connect with the company's chief customers and suppliers before you even consider making an offer.

Buying Into a Franchise

A franchise is a license to own or operate a branch of an existing business using the name, logo, and business model that have already been proven successful. Subway, McDonald's, and Anytime Fitness are examples of franchise businesses. Be aware that while franchises have a better success rate than brand-new start-up companies, they are not guaranteed to succeed; even successful franchises have branches that fail.

Franchise ownership is different from independent business ownership on many levels. On one hand, franchise owners get the benefit of having an established name under which to start their business. This can help make sales happen faster from the outset. When starting a business with a name that already has a good reputation, you'll probably have to put in less work selling potential clients on your business. Also, franchise ownership usually comes with a built-in support system, via corporate headquarters and other franchise owners. This can be helpful, as you'll have a large network of people with previous experience in the company that can help you overcome hurdles as you build your store. Third, obtaining financing for franchise businesses is often easier than obtaining financing for start-up businesses that have no prior track record.

On the other hand, franchise businesses require that you play by the company rules. Franchise agreements often allow little variances for creativity in business ownership and expansion as they have rules for how things are to be run. Also, with most franchise companies, a portion of your profit goes directly to the franchise headquarters. Third, franchisers are often not required to renew your contract at the end of the specified term, meaning there is a risk you could lose your business if it's not performing up to the franchiser's expectations.

Once you've expressed serious interest in opening a franchise, the franchiser (the company) will send you a franchise disclosure document (FDD), required by the Federal Trade Commission (FTC). This crucial document has twenty-three required parts, and it's important to read them all thoroughly to make sure you fully understand both your and the franchiser's roles and responsibilities.

Here is some basic information to find before buying into an existing franchise:

- How long the company has been in business
- The buy-in and other fees associated with purchasing this franchise
- Available financing options

- The amount of operating capital typically necessary to carry the franchise until the breakeven point
- When the average franchise owner with your company breaks even
- Revenue, profitability statistics, and success/failure rate of typical franchise owners
- The territory for this franchise, and whether other franchise owners can move into the territory
- Contact information for current franchise owners
- What supports the company offers for advertising, promotion, and business coaching
- The company's rules and regulations for franchise owners

Most franchise owners want to make their franchise business successful enough that they don't have to run it themselves. Instead, they work to hire a team that will eventually run things for them. Therefore when looking to purchase a franchise, it may be wise to pick a nationally recognizable business that has a low up-front cost. By having a clear picture of how an existing business runs before you make a purchasing decision, you can be sure to have clearer expectations of what will happen after you own part or all of the business.

Starting Your Own Business

Some people fund their ERP by starting their own business. There are endless possibilities for doing this. There are passive income businesses such as owning websites and using them to create income via affiliate marketing, ad networks, or products sold online via links to other sites (sales on which you receive a commission). There are also active businesses such as engineering firms, landscaping companies, or other types of companies that will require day-to-day hands-on work from you or the employees you hire. There are several things you can consider that will help you figure out what type of business may be right for you.

Do you want a business you can run yourself or with a team, or do you want a passive, hands-off business that you can hire others to run? Even if you want a passive business you will have to spend some time running or helping to run the business at first.

It's also important to take a personal skills and talent inventory. By making a list of your skills and talents you can narrow the field of what type of business you can start. Are you a technical person who is great at IT or computer stuff? Are you a creative person who is good at writing, marketing, or art? Are you a service person, gifted at providing great service to others? What types of people do you work best with? Are you good at teaching others? Are you good at organization?

Think about whether you have the necessary skills to market and promote a business; if not, are you willing to learn them? Probably the most difficult part of any business start-up is getting the word out about the products and/or services you offer. It's important to have a plan for promotion and advertising before you start a business.

Make sure you have a clear understanding of what's involved with starting and owning a business. The first years are usually filled with a lot of hard work. A passive role can often come only after years of growing and establishing your business. Are you prepared to do what it takes to get the business running well?

Creating a business plan can be a good place to start to help you determine whether or not a specific business may be right for you. It will take some time for you to write a business plan for your potential business. A good business plan includes eight basic components:

1. **Executive summary.** This is a snapshot of your business, including your goals for the business and information about the company profile. A company profile is a summary that includes your business history, organizational management structure, and past and current performance numbers.

2. **Company description.** The company description is a more expansive picture of what your company does, the type of business entity (LLC or S corporation, for example), who its client base is, what markets your business targets, and what differentiates your business from other similar businesses.

3. **Market analysis.** The market analysis contains a thorough description of your target audience and market, specific information about potential competitors, information about the industry itself, your projected sales, and how you'll overcome hurdles.

4. **Organization and management.** This section of your business plan includes information on how your business will be managed, who will have what responsibilities, and an outline of who will fulfill what roles and what makes them qualified to do so.

5. **Service or product line.** This section tells the story about what your business does. What are you selling and how will it benefit your customers? What is the life cycle of the product or business, and how will you keep customers coming back?

6. **Marketing and sales.** How do you plan on getting the word out about your business? How will you find potential clients, and what tactics will you use to convince them that your product or service is beneficial to them?

7. **Funding request.** How much money do you need to buy or start your business? What are your funding requirements for the

next five years? How do you intend to use the money for the business? When writing this section, include how much money you'll need now, how much you'll need in the future, the type of funding you would like to have, and how much of your own cash you will be contributing to the venture. Make sure to include the amount of money you'll need to live on until the business starts bringing in enough cash and profits to support you.

8. **Financial projections.** This section should include specific financial information for each of the next five years of your business, including how much you expect to earn via sales, your anticipated expense amounts, and why you expect those numbers to work.

For more specific information on how to write a business plan, check out this government website: www.sba.gov/business-guide/plan/write-your-business-plan-template.

Business Debt

You also need to figure out whether or not you will need to take out a loan to start the business. A business plan is essential if you expect to try to gain financing for your business. Business debt can be helpful—if your business is successful. The problem with taking on business debt is that, according to *Inc.*, one of the world's largest business magazines, 96 percent of all businesses fail within ten years.

Many people have gone into serious debt in order to start a business—and lost it all. Starting and running a business with debt means that business will have to bring in extra income to cover the debt payments each month. Covering that debt payment puts your business at risk of not being able to cover payroll and other expenses. This can affect not just your family but the families of anyone on your payroll as well.

If you want to have your own business there are many ways to do that without going into debt. A business failure that's paid for with cash is tough, but a business failure that leaves you tens or hundreds of thousands of dollars in debt is a whole other ball game. It could take away any chance you have to retire early as you work your job to pay back that debt. Starting and growing your business with cash will help you ensure you always have money to make payroll as you hire employees and stay solvent as you grow your business. It is possible to start a business without debt. Here is one example.

Case Study: David Starts a Business Without Debt

With a good knowledge of website design, David decided to start a business designing websites for small businesses. David determined start-up costs for equipment would run roughly $3,500 based on his research of the industry. Since he didn't want to pay to rent office space, he decided to meet with local clients at their places of business and focus on meeting via Skype with businesses that were farther away.

David did his first ten basic website designs for $500 each in order to build his portfolio and his list of references. After the first year, David was able to increase his prices.

David worked hard in those first years on building his business. He searched the Internet for companies whose websites were less than ideal. He made cold calls both in person in his local urban area and online to out-of-state company owners. In the first two years he worked sixty or more hours a week gaining clients and designing their sites. He advertised in local papers and attended local networking events, building relationships with local business owners. He also had to spend time assuring his clients paid on time and calling clients who didn't pay on time.

After five years of designing sites and working on advertising his business, David now has two full-time employees and serves dozens of clients each year with their website-related needs. Although it was not easy and involved sixty- to seventy-hour weeks, it is getting him closer to his goal of early retirement. He rents a nice but affordable storefront where he and his staff can meet with clients. By building his business slowly he's been able to pay cash as he goes and has never taken out debt for his business.

David's business is able to run largely on its own thanks to good hiring choices and David spends roughly fifteen to twenty hours a week meeting with clients and his employees, but he takes a salary of $60,000 from his business since his business is set up as an S corp. He chose the business structure so that he could take a base salary at a normal tax rate and then any bonuses above that would be paid out as dividends and taxed at capital gains rates, which is traditionally lower.

Choosing any business venture wisely is important, as is paying any start-up costs with cash you have saved as you fund your ERP. There are many businesses that can help you produce a consistent monthly income as they become more profitable over time. See Appendix C for some examples of businesses you can start—and grow—using cash only.

Costs and Risks

With any business purchase there are costs involved. It's important to be well aware of these costs before you make the move into business ownership.

Every business costs money to get off the ground—these are its start-up costs. You may need to spend money purchasing a building, buying supplies and equipment, or hiring staff. You will also need money to cover recurring costs until your business begins making a profit. It's important to be aware of what start-up and ongoing costs are applicable to the business you are considering.

Every business venture involves risks. Slow growth, higher-than-anticipated expenses, staff problems, product defects, and unhappy customers are some of the potential problems that can come with business ownership. Make sure you have a plan for what those risks might be and how you will overcome them.

An Exit Strategy

Smart business owners also develop an exit strategy. Maybe your goal is to run your business for a few years and then hand off daily operations to someone else. Or maybe your goal is to sell the business after ten years. Whatever your vision, it is important to develop your exit strategy before you buy into your business. Develop different exit strategies, as you never know how things will play out as the years go on. Whereas you initially might plan to still own the business while handing off day-to-day operations, that might change after a few years and you may want to sell the business outright. Having a few different exit strategies on hand will help you to account for different scenarios that may come into play.

For instance, one exit strategy could be to hire a competent and experienced manager with the goal of training him to eventually take your place as CEO while you take on the role of silent business owner only. Once that person is trained in, you could try leaving the daily business responsibilities for a time as you analyze how the business runs without you.

Another exit strategy could be to sell the business outright after you reach a certain number of years of ownership or after the business reaches a certain value.

The goal is to make the business a profitable one—one where you get a monthly paycheck even though you're now doing little or no work to run the business, and living off a monthly paycheck or the funds you gained when you sold the business.

Business Investing Returns

Investing in small and medium-sized businesses has the potential to produce a sizable return, but because most businesses fail within the first ten years, it's important to choose your business investments wisely. According to a study done by Sageworks, the average ROE (return on equity) for a small business in a high-return industry (mainly professional services such as legal, medical, accounting, and brokerage) was 39.10 percent, which is a phenomenal return. Obviously, most small businesses will not see that kind of return, and they qualify as high-risk investments. However, building or buying into a business in which you already have experience and knowledge will substantially increase your chances of success.

Other Investment Options

There are a few other investing options aside from the three main ones we have discussed in this chapter. However, many of them have consistently low returns or have higher risk attached to them. For instance, consider gold and ten-year Treasury bills, generally considered very low-risk investments, when compared to the stock and real estate markets.

Gold

Although in the past gold has performed fairly well as far as ROI, the Dow Jones Industrial Average and the S&P 500 still beat both gold and the Treasury bill returns over the long haul (which makes sense, because both of those investments have historically low risk of loss). There have been long periods when gold hasn't appreciated in value at all and T-bills have taken a drastic dive in returns. So don't expect investing solely in these options to provide the returns necessary to retire early, though (in small amounts) they may add some stability to an otherwise high-risk portfolio.

Individual Stocks

Buying stocks in only a few companies can be risky as well. If one (or both) of those companies fail, you'll lose a huge portion (or all) of your ERP money. Investing in the broad portions of the market through index or other funds—such as mutual funds or exchange-traded funds—lets you own shares in many different companies, thereby minimizing the risk of total loss.

Collectibles

While some investors prefer collectibles (such as wine, stamps, and art) because of the tangibility of assets, the appreciation potential on those types of investments is typically less than what you can earn by investing in the stock market instead. The other risk with investing in collectibles is their illiquidity, meaning it may be hard to find a buyer if and when you're ready to sell.

Annuities

Another commonly proposed investment option for retirement is the annuity, which comes in a few different forms and can have very complicated features. Often, advisers that sell them don't dwell on the fact that many annuities offer low guaranteed rates of return and may involve high fees, especially if you want to sell them and get your money back. The right annuities can make sense in specific circumstances, but it's important to do some research on the types of annuities you're considering before putting any of your hard-earned cash into them.

Hire a Financial Adviser or Go It Alone?

While some people argue you should hire an adviser to help choose and manage stock market investments, others believe firmly in managing investment accounts on their own. In the end the choice has to be your own, but there are two important questions to ask yourself that will help you to decide whether or not you should hire a financial adviser to assist you with choosing and managing your investments.

1. *How much do I know about investing and financial planning?* The less you know about these subjects, the more valuable a financial adviser may be to you as you plan how you will grow your ERP investments. Advisers are trained to help clients choose investments that will help them accomplish their financial goals.
2. *Do I want to spend the time to manage my own investments?* Even if you know a lot about investing, you may not have the time or want to spend the time to be your own financial adviser. Understanding the world of investing and financial management is a time-consuming endeavor.

Before hiring an adviser, it's important to know which certifications and how much experience she or he has in the field. The Certified Financial Planner (CFP) designation is becoming more important for people hiring a financial planner. To obtain a CFP designation, an adviser needs to pass a series of tests and meet strict experience requirements. Looking for this qualification will help you weed out the less serious advisers and hire a more educated adviser. To find out if an adviser has a CFP designation, you can check by searching here: www.letsmakeaplan.org.

There are a couple of other designations you may come across as you search for an adviser to help you with early retirement planning.

A personal financial specialist (PFS) is a certified public accountant (CPA) with additional credentials that focus on personal financial planning. A CPA with PFS status should be qualified to help a person with comprehensive financial planning questions. A chartered financial analyst (CFA) has been certified by the CFA Institute, an organization that measures the competence and integrity of financial analysts. Although a person with a CFA designation does know a lot about money, this isn't someone you would normally use to help you manage your personal finances.

It's important to question potential financial advisers before making the decision to hire one. Although longevity/experience isn't always an indicator of a sound adviser, it could give you an idea of that person's experience level when it comes to investing and managing money. Also, a financial adviser should be willing to give potential clients a list of references that can vouch for his performance. If he is not willing to share references, it might be a good idea to move on to another adviser.

Here are some good questions to ask:

- *Are you a fee-only adviser or fee-based adviser?* A fee-only adviser charges only a flat annual fee for maintaining your investment account. A fee-based adviser also gets commissions based on which products he sells.

- *If you are a fee-only adviser, what is your annual fee?* Many experts say that 1 percent of your total assets invested with the adviser is a fair fee.

- *Can you give me a list of references?* It's perfectly acceptable to ask a financial adviser for references as to his or her performance.

- *What is your experience and background in the financial field?* It's important for you to feel comfortable with an adviser's level of experience.

- *What licenses or professional certifications do you hold?* Knowing which credentials the professional holds gives you assurances about his competency level, plus you can easily check to make sure his credentials remain in good standing.

- *What services will you and won't you provide for the discussed fee amount?* It's wise to be clear on exactly what you are—and aren't—getting for the fee that you pay your financial adviser.

- *Will my money be held with a third-party custodian?* Invested funds are safer from fraud when the adviser doesn't hold the funds. A third-party custodian is a trusted financial company such as Charles Schwab, Scottrade, or Vanguard.

- *What is your process for helping clients determine investment needs and choices?* A good adviser will ask many questions about a client's investment goals and needs, current financial situation, risk tolerance, and lifestyle, and listen intently to the answers before making investment recommendations.

- *What types of clients do you normally serve?* If you are in a situation where you have a small lump sum (less than $2,500, for example) to invest and want to add a few hundred dollars a month to your investment account, an adviser who generally works with wealthy clients and million-dollar portfolios may not be the best choice for you.

By interviewing more than one adviser and by asking questions regarding all of your concerns, you can increase the likelihood that your relationship with your financial adviser will be a happy one.

Keep in mind that adviser fees are separate from trading fees and mutual fund expenses. Those costs will also impact how much of your investment earnings contribute to your ERP.

Robo-Advisers

In Chapter 2 we talked briefly about robo-advisers. A robo-adviser doesn't leave you fully on your own to manage investments, but doesn't have the full hands-on help that some investors seek. Robo-advisers are becoming increasingly popular with investors as they look to minimize investment fees that impact wealth growth. Whereas most financial advisers typically charge at least 1 percent of your annual balance (and potentially more if they are fee-based), robo-advisers generally charge around 0.25 percent to 0.50 percent of your investment balance.

Two examples of companies that specialize in using robo-advisers are Betterment and Wealthfront.

Betterment offers three basic programs for investors. Their basic program charges a 0.25 percent annual fee and doesn't carry a minimum balance. It offers automated portfolio management and investment advice. Betterment's Plus Plan requires a $100,000 minimum account balance and charges a 0.40 percent annual fee. It offers one annual call with their team of licensed financial experts as well as additional monitoring of your accounts throughout the year. The company's Premium membership requires a $250,000 minimum balance and charges a 0.50 percent annual fee, still much lower than traditional investment firms. The Premium membership allows for unlimited calls with their team of certified financial planners and other licensed financial experts. Betterment also has the added benefit of no additional fees for trades or transactions—your annual fee covers everything. The annual fees are also prorated, so if for some reason you cancel your Betterment account early you'll get a partial refund of your fee payment.

Wealthfront runs on the same concept but the terms are a bit different. They manage the first $10,000 you invest with them at no cost. After that the management fee is 0.25 percent. The minimum account balance is $500. There are no additional fees with Wealthfront, and they offer options for investing in retirement accounts, nonretirement accounts, and college savings accounts. As a bonus for lower-balance investors, they'll manage an additional $5,000 for free if you get a friend to sign up for their robo-investing services.

Both Betterment and Wealthfront are great options for investing when you don't want to use a traditional investment firm. Annual costs are much lower with robo-advisers such as these, and they're great for investors who have some idea of what they are doing in the investing world.

Case Study: Michael and Amanda Invest in the Stock Market

Michael is twenty-nine and Amanda is twenty-eight. Michael works as an electrician and earns $65,000 per year. Amanda is a personal loan specialist at a bank and earns $50,000 per year. They want to retire in twenty years. They don't have children but plan on having them in the future. Michael and Amanda decide to live off Michael's income and invest Amanda's. Their goal is to have $4,000 per month to live on during retirement.

If Michael and Amanda invest her take-home pay of $2,800 per month in an investment account that earns 8 percent returns and invest for twenty years, they'll build an investment account balance of

$1,603,448 (based on a model that assumes they deposit exactly that amount every month for twenty years and never take any money out of the account).

Remember in Chapter 1 we mentioned that investments should be switched to a lower-risk investment after retirement, because the purpose of the return postretirement is security and not growth. So if Michael and Amanda maintain a 4 percent ROI after retirement by switching to less risky investments, they'll still have more than a million dollars in their investment account after thirty years of withdrawals if they withdraw $5,000 every month, which will include $4,000 for their monthly living expenses and $1,000 for any taxes they might have to pay. This will give them enough money to live on well into their nineties and to account for any market fluctuations as well as inflation costs of 3 percent a year.

Investing—especially in index funds and mutual funds—has proven over the decades to be a solid path to wealth accumulation; however, it is important to understand the potential fees involved and make sure that you aren't paying more than you have to in fees and losing money in this area. Thousands of early retirees and self-made millionaires have found investing, real estate ownership, and business ownership to be successful routes to financial independence. Although these three investments aren't the only avenues for funding your ERP, they all have proven (but not guaranteed) success in growing wealth. As you determine how you will fund your postretirement lifestyle, I encourage you to consider using one or more of these investment strategies to produce at least some of your ERP income.

CHAPTER 8

Stick with the Plan

Probably the most difficult part of achieving early retirement is sticking with the plan. This is where most people get off track and give up. Goals that take a long time to achieve are tough to stay with. If you want to make it to the finish line and complete your ERP, you're going to have to know what you need to do in order to stick with the plan.

There are a few things that can get you off track and lull you into giving up on your early retirement goals. The following outlines potential temptations and what you can do to avoid them.

Get-Rich-Quick Schemes and Scams

As you build your wealth slowly and steadily through real estate, investing, or business ownership, temptations to get to your goal faster are going to show up on the radar. Many times these temptations are in the form of "get-rich-quick" schemes.

You've probably seen infomercials or had loved ones ask you to share in an "opportunity" that promises fast money. It's easy to be lured into getting involved with scams like this. Who doesn't want to make a lot of money in a short amount of time?

The problem is that most of these scams aren't what they promise to be. So, how can you spot a legit money-making opportunity over a get-rich-quick scheme?

Signs of a Get-Rich-Quick Scam

Get-rich-quick scams have a few different markers that make them stand out. First, they'll promise what seem to be too-good-to-be-true results. If someone says you'll have to do very little work and will earn a large amount of cash or a large profit in very little time, they're probably trying to scam you.

Many get-rich-quick schemes focus on the hype instead of the product or service. They'll spend a lot of time talking about you and your dreams. They'll make statements that play on your emotions, such as, "Are you tired of being broke all the time? Do you dream of having a mansion and playing golf all day? Of traveling the world and having no money worries?"

They'll give you a lot of information about the people who are making a large income through their company but they won't spend much time focusing on their product or service.

A get-rich-quick scheme may have a product or plan that is unproven. Also, some schemes don't actually sell a product; instead they sell membership into the company as the primary source of income. If a company is promoting recruiting members as the primary way to make money, that's a sign of an illegitimate business—a classic pyramid scheme.

A scam offer may ask you to pay in a large amount of money up front—or make a large purchase of their products.

If you see any of these signs in a business you are considering, do thorough research before investing a dime.

Signs of a Legit Money-Making Opportunity

Just as there are signs that indicate an offer is a scam, there are those that indicate a legit money-making business.

First, a legitimate business will focus on a specific product or service. Second, it will have a proven track record and long-term history. Third, the money needed to get started in the business will make sense and not break your budget. However, even with a legitimate company it's important to choose carefully before getting involved in any business opportunity.

A Word about Multilevel Marketing Companies

Multilevel marketing (MLM) companies have long gotten a bad rap—and with good reason. For those of you not familiar with these, multilevel marketing companies, also known as network marketing, are companies that use a pyramid-shaped marketing strategy. This consists of profits from selling direct to customers and from commissions for recruiting team members. Many less-than-ethical MLMs have come and gone over the years and have taken advantage of well-meaning people. However, there are also some good MLMs out there: Mary Kay, Pampered Chef, and Herbalife, for example. Before you choose an MLM as a way to increase your income for the purposes of early retirement, it's wise to ask yourself some important questions:

- *Do I believe in the company and its product 100 percent?* The people who succeed in legitimate MLMs have a true passion for the products or services they sell. If you don't believe that the products or services you are selling have a benefit for potential buyers, you'll have a tough time convincing people to buy from you. You'll have an even tougher time convincing people to join your team, which counts for a large portion of the income successful MLM reps make.

- *Is the product they sell beneficial to a wide range of people?* A successful MLM company will have a product or service that will appeal to the masses. The more specific the product is, the less opportunity you'll have to sell it.
- *Can I grow my business without the help of family and friends?* Many relationships have gone sour due to the relentless sales pitches of well-meaning MLM reps to family and friends. If you are going to start an MLM business, be sure you have the sales and marketing skills that will allow you to grow your business without much mention of it to family and friends. Most successful MLM reps do well because they are good at cold-call sales to complete strangers.
- *What is the lifespan of the company?* The best MLM opportunities exist in companies with a long lifespan. The longer their products or services have been on the market, the more solid the opportunity is.
- *Am I prepared financially and mentally for failure?* It's smart to have a positive attitude when going into any business; however, you must also be prepared to accept failure if it doesn't work out. With most MLMs, if the company disappears or if your personal business fails you walk away with nothing. That's 100 percent loss. In my experience, MLMs are not the way to go when looking to retire early. Very few people make a substantial income in the MLM industry, often because of the bad reputation of the industry in general. Stand-alone businesses that offer solid services or products are more likely to be respected.

The Lottery

Americans spent more than $70 billion on lottery tickets in 2014. What is the likelihood of winning?

Winning big jackpots like the Powerball is highly unlikely; a recent Powerball drawing disclaimer stated that the chance of winning the big jackpot was 1 in 292 million. How unlikely is a 1 in 292 million chance of winning? Your chances of being struck by falling airplane parts are over twenty-nine times higher at one in 10 million. Your chances of being killed by lightning are a over hundred times higher at one in 2.3 million.

What if, on the other hand, a regular lottery player took the $300 a year he spends on tickets and invested it in the stock market? If he started at $0 and invested $25 a month over a period of thirty years at 8 percent, he'd have $36,703 in an investment account. Although that may not seem like a lot of cash, it could fund many peoples' early retirement plans for a year or even two.

So, you have a choice: you can spend your $25 a month on a 1 in 292 million chance of winning the big jackpot, or you can bet on the proven historical returns of the stock market instead and fund your retirement life for a couple of years.

The Casino

Another popular method of attempting to get rich quick is through casino gambling. There are many different games available for play at the casino, but for the purpose of simplicity let's talk about slot machines. Here's what Casino.org has to say about the odds of winning on slot machines:

> "Slots have one of the highest house edges to be found in the casino (typically over 7 percent) and because you can play

a large number of turns very quickly [it] makes slots nearly impossible to win money on over the long term."

Contrary to popular opinion, the article reports, a player's odds don't improve when he plays the machine for a longer time. Instead, each turn presents the same odds, and there is no set order of payout cycles.

On the other hand, saving and investing the money you would have played at the casino could have a much higher rate of return: 11.42 percent (average annual returns) on the S&P 500 from 1928–2016, 3.46 percent on a three-month Treasury bill during that same period, and 5.18 percent on a ten-year Treasury bond over that same period.

Get-rich-quick schemes, the lottery, and the casino can all be tempting avenues for attempting to achieve your target ERP number faster, but the odds show that reaching your early retirement goals through these methods will likely result in money loss and not gain. Stick with the tried-and-true methods that have worked for thousands of now-wealthy people, and give yourself a much higher chance of early retirement success.

Why Perseverance Matters

The best plans in the world for early retirement won't do you any good if you're not willing to persevere. In my opinion, this is the toughest part of completing your early retirement goal. Why? One word: distractions.

As soon as you create your ERP and take that first step to start achieving your goal, distractions and temptations will start to come your way. Following are some of the types of distractions you might face and how you can overcome them to achieve your ERP goal.

Temptations to Keep Up with the Joneses

Once you change your lifestyle and decide that achieving the wealth necessary for early retirement is more important to you than owning stuff, the Joneses will come knocking at your door with their "You only live once" message.

The Joneses might come in the form of well-meaning family and friends, jealous onlookers, cunning advertising and marketing, or as messages from your own mind. People who don't understand your goal might pity you for living below your means or may assume your lack of spending means you must have money troubles.

They might ridicule your frugal ways. They might even be offended when you turn down offers to go out to dinner or on a vacation. It is normal human nature to want to fit in with others and to be hurt or even scared when others reject or criticize you, and it's important to be prepared for negative reactions from others as you start taking the steps you need to take to increase your net worth for the purposes of early retirement.

Giving Your Kids "The Best of Everything"

No one will argue the point that kids can be expensive. The latest studies show that it costs more than $230,000 to raise a child from birth through high school graduation.

Raising kids can put a serious dent in your ability to retire early, but by setting down some ground rules and considering these options for frugal child-rearing, parents can achieve their financial goals and give their kids a great life at the same time.

Weigh Income Against Childcare Expenses

One of the most expensive parts of parenting is paying for childcare for kids who aren't yet of school age. But a two-income family doesn't always mean more money in the family pocketbook. Sometimes—depending on each parent's income potential—it's actually cheaper to have one parent stay home and raise the kids until they're in school. Work-from-home careers are also an option for parents who want to stay home with their kids. Many work-from-home jobs such as freelancing and customer service–based jobs allow parents to set their own hours so that they can work around their family's schedule.

When deciding whether it's more beneficial to your family for both parents to work or whether one will stay home, be sure to take into account the net amount of the lowest spousal income. After subtracting work-related expenses such as transportation, clothing, and meals and what you pay for childcare, you might find your bank account is better off if one parent stays home.

Be Selective about Extracurricular Activities

It's tempting for parents to allow their kids to participate in every activity under the sun, but the costs of extracurricular activities can be a large part of child-rearing expenses. Instead of allowing your kids to take part in every activity that comes along, have them pick the one or two activities per year that mean the most to them or that provide the best long-term benefit. By keeping extracurricular activities to a minimum you'll not only save tens of thousands of dollars, but you'll enjoy a less stressful life as well due to a lighter schedule for the kids.

Never Pay Full Price

Even if you insist on your kids only wearing name-brand clothes and shoes there's no reason to ever have to pay full price. Store sales, consignment stores, garage sales, Facebook group sales, and online sites such as eBay all offer quality kids' clothes for a fraction of full retail price. If you're willing to dress your kids in basic big-box store clothing, you can save even more.

As an aside, your infant or toddler won't have a clue if what he's wearing fits in with the latest fashions, so if you are set on outfitting your kids in name-brand clothing, consider saving money by waiting until they're old enough to care.

The same goes for toys, cribs, bicycles, and other kid gear. Clearance sales and sale-by-owner opportunities mean there's always a good deal on kids' gear waiting around the corner for those willing to be patient.

Stick to a Grocery Budget

Grocery bills account for one of the biggest expenses when it comes to raising kids. The United States Department of Agriculture reports that the average family of four (two parents and two children between ages six and eleven) spends between $636.70 and $1,268.70 a month on groceries. However, it is possible to spend less on groceries by following some tried-and-true grocery shopping rules.

- **Make a menu plan:** Menu plans are a vital part of any frugal grocery budget. When you plan out the week's meals beforehand and create your shopping list to coordinate with the menu, you avoid the "nothing in the house" excuse that causes people to order pizza or head out to restaurants to eat. Plus, there are meals that can be bought and served for somewhere in the $5 per serving range.
- **Shop for sales:** Make your menu plan based on what's on sale for the week. If chicken is on special, have a few different chicken-based meals during the week. If apples are on sale, make that your fruit of choice for the week. By shopping the sales you can make sure you're getting the best deal on groceries.

- **Avoid convenience foods:** Snack foods, junk foods, and other convenience foods are bad for your health and for your pocketbook. Stick to whole foods, drink water instead of soda, and make desserts from scratch in order to save money on your grocery bill.
- **Know your prices:** Knowing the prices of grocery items you buy regularly will help you spot good deals. By memorizing or keeping a list of the prices of items you buy regularly, you can get the best deal on those items and avoid paying more than you need to.
- **Avoid unplanned stops at the store:** Unplanned grocery trips can ruin a grocery budget. Make a plan to shop once a week and then get what you need, rather than popping into the store to satisfy a craving.

By using these tips you may be able to cut down your grocery bill substantially.

FEEDING A FAMILY OF FOUR

If you think it is tough to reduce your grocery budget, be sure to check out how Erin Chase fed her family of four on $250 per month here: http://wellkeptwallet.com/72-how-to-cut-your-grocery-budget-in-half-with-erin-chase/.

Look for Affordable Education Options

Education costs for kids are another potential roadblock to early retirement. Many people aren't happy with the public education available where they live, so they choose to spend the money on a private education for their children. However, private education tuition can be costly. If education costs are hindering your ability to fund your ERP, consider some of the following education alternatives for your children.

Is it possible to move to a public school district that you're happier with, or to take advantage of an open enrollment situation that will allow your kids to attend better schools? If you need to move to do so, remember to take into account housing costs in the school district you're considering moving to so that your new housing costs don't hinder your ERP plans. Sometimes homes in better school districts can cost more, so it's important before making a move for schooling purposes to consider options that won't hinder your ERP due to more housing debt. If you are set on living in a better school district, you may need to consider living in a smaller home that costs less to offset the difference in housing costs so that you don't have less money available to save for early retirement.

Some school districts have excellent charter schools that allow for a higher-grade education than what their public schools offer. Language, math, and science charter schools are common in today's world. Is there a charter school option for your kids that will allow them a better education yet not affect your pocketbook?

You can also consider homeschooling. Some parents and children might do well in a homeschooling situation if they're not happy with the public education system where they live but can't afford private schooling. Homeschooling does cost money; however it can be done frugally. For instance, Laurie, who blogs at *The Frugal Farmer*, homeschooled her four kids in 2016 for a total of just over $3,200. In the years prior to that she spent much less to homeschool all four children. Homeschooling parents have the option to choose curricula that fits in with their budget as long as that curricula is acceptable by their state's homeschool requirements. Also, many school districts allow homeschooled students to participate in public school extracurricular activities and sports. Local homeschooling co-ops often have sports programs that are much less expensive than other private or community-run programs. Although not free, homeschooling can be a much less expensive option than many private schools cost. Sites such as HSLDA.org can tell you more about what to expect when considering homeschooling your children.

Another education expense that can come with having children is college tuition. If you start planning early for your children's college tuition fees you can make sure those costs don't inhibit your plans to retire early.

Decide ahead of time how much you'll contribute to those college costs. A paid-for college education isn't a requirement for parents to their children. Decide early on (and make it clear to your children early) what—if any—amount of money you will contribute toward their college education.

Parents can contribute toward a child's education in other ways as well, such as by letting them live at home for free and providing their meals if they attend a local college. Decide how much you will contribute and make a plan in your budget that will allow you to fund early retirement as well as help your kids with college as you've determined.

If you start saving money for your child's college education as soon as she or he is born, the monthly amount you'll need to save to achieve your college fund goals will be smaller. Plus, the sooner you start saving, the more time your money has to grow, thanks to the magic of compound returns (where you earn more money on the earnings you've already gained). That means you could put away less money, but still end up with a bigger college fund than if you'd started saving later.

There are several ways you can help your kids minimize what it costs to get a degree. Help them research the different schooling options, available scholarships, and credit transfer information that will help them reduce tuition and other costs as they decide where and when to go to college. Kids can generally start working at age fifteen or sixteen in most states. By encouraging your children to find income sources and start saving early, you can help them minimize student loan needs.

Focus on What Your Kids Really Need

More than the latest and greatest toys and gadgets, what kids truly desire is quality and quantity time with their parents. If you can make this a priority in your parenting, you'll likely find that your kids' need for "stuff" diminishes immensely. Yes, kids can be expensive. However, parents can also minimize the amount of money they spend on kids by making wise decisions.

Nevertheless, it's not always possible to reduce your child-rearing expenses down to a bare-bones budget. Circumstances such as chronic illness or special needs situations can add tens of thousands of dollars to a child-rearing budget, even if you take all the steps suggested previously to cut costs. Therefore it is important to remember that raising children will likely have a noticeable impact on your ERP and to take the necessary steps to allow for that impact.

Constant Technological Upgrades

Today's technological world can be tough on the pocketbook. New smartphones, laptops, and other tech gadgets arrive on the market regularly, and if you fall for the "gotta have" mentality regarding tech gadgets, you can easily spend thousands of dollars per year on unnecessary upgrades.

Learn to be content with what you have and don't fall for the lie that you have to keep up with the Joneses in the area of tech gadgets.

Creating an Environment That Helps You Achieve Your Plan

Besides avoiding temptations to abandon your early retirement plan, there are things you can do to keep moving forward. Remembering your *why*, reengaging with your plan, revisiting your goals, and adding mini-goals into your plan can help you to stay on track when you're feeling discouraged and considering abandoning your plan.

Remember Your *Why*

This step can't be stressed enough. At the beginning of this book when you created your *why* chart, you were probably pretty excited about the thought of being able to retire early. By regularly revisiting your chart or poster board, you can revive the excitement that helped you create your plan in the first place.

Work to visualize why you want to retire early and all the things you'll do once you can retire. Remind yourself regularly why you want out of the rat race and into a life where you make your own daily decisions. Revisit your plan every time you are tempted to give up and get motivated to keep going.

Reengage with Your Plan

Sometimes working on your ERP is going to get boring. You'll get tired of saving money and not spending like everyone else is. Reengaging with your plan can help overcome that boredom and get you motivated again. Here's how to do that.

Revisit Your Goals

Go over your to-do list for early retirement again. See if you are on track, and work to find areas where you might have gotten off track. If you're doing well at keeping with the plan, great. If you're not, you might need to change up your goals or the way you get your goals accomplished.

Create Mini-Goals

Sometimes it's easier to reengage with your plan if you break down some of your ERP goals into smaller pieces. For instance, let's say that one of your ERP goals is to pay off your mortgage. You still have $150,000 left to go and it seems like it's taking forever to get to your goal.

Make mini-goals that will help it seem like you are getting there faster. Create a chart with 150 squares on it and put "$1,000" in each square. Work to pay off your mortgage faster by finding more income or selling things you own. Every time you pay $1,000 off on your mortgage, you can put an X, a sticker, or some other victory sign on one of those $1,000 squares. Put some fun and excitement into your plan that will help keep you engaged with each step.

Ignore the Naysayers

Unfortunately, not everyone will support your decision to retire early. You are planning to do something extraordinary, and extraordinary plans are often met with resistance from family and friends. Some may criticize your decision to create wealth and retire early. You might get pushback as you cut expenses and start managing your money differently.

There are generally two types of naysayers whom people come across as they begin working their ERP plan: "crabs in a bucket" and "monkeys in a cage."

If you put a crab in a bucket it will surely try to escape. However, if you put two or more crabs in a bucket, any crab that tries to escape will be pulled down by the other crabs. It's the "If I can't have it, neither can you" syndrome. As you work your ERP you might come across some people who feel this way about your early retirement plan. They might ridicule your frugality or your goal of retiring before sixty-five, telling you that it is unrealistic. The truth is that they may be feeling threatened at the thought of you leaving them behind financially or upset at their own financial shortcomings.

In a behavioral study five monkeys were put in a cage with a tall ceiling. In the middle of the cage was a pole, and at the top of the pole was a bunch of bananas. However, each time a monkey tried to climb the pole to get the bananas, the scientists sprayed it with a powerful stream of water, and the monkey would run back down to the cage floor. Over time all five monkeys had tried to get the bananas and been sprayed with water. They learned to not climb up the pole—a logical reaction given their experience. What happened next was interesting. One by one, the monkeys were replaced with new monkeys. Each time a new monkey tried to climb the pole, the other monkeys would pull him down, trying fervently to save him from getting blasted with water.

Eventually, all original five monkeys who had been sprayed with water were replaced, and all of the monkeys that were now in the cage had not yet been sprayed with water. However, each time a monkey would try to climb the pole and get the bananas, the others would pull him down, not even knowing why. It was just "what everyone did."

TALK IT OUT

If you decide to reduce expenses in the areas of gift giving, travel, and entertainment, loved ones might feel rejected, hurt, or judged. You can help calm their fears by assuring them that your decision to do life differently doesn't change how you feel about them.

In the first story about the crabs, the intention of the crabs was self-serving; they didn't want others to get ahead of them. In the second story, the monkeys were merely trying to save their fellow monkey from trouble.

In your life, you might have naysayers who are working to talk you out of achieving your ERP for their own selfish purposes. Or you might encounter naysayers who sincerely believe you are short-changing yourself by living a frugal life in exchange for a better one down the road.

The "crabs" in your life might make fun of you and your out-of-the-park savings rate. The "monkeys" might sincerely feel bad that you "have to" drive an older car—even if that car is reliable and fits your needs just fine.

Minimizing talk about your ERP may help as well. A good general rule to consider is to not talk about your ERP unless someone asks and is genuinely interested. Trying to convince those you love to join you on the road to financial independence probably won't work unless they decide on their own that they want it and then come to you for advice.

It's important not to let naysayers bring you down. Work to minimize stress in your relationships with the naysayers in your life, and be confident that eventually your current relationships will adjust. Even better, you will also find new friends who share your goal of financial independence. Your new relationships with those on a similar path to yours will give you an outlet for the excitement you have about reaching your goal of early retirement.

Get an Accountability Partner

We talked briefly about this in the beginning of the book but I'd like to expand on the topic. Whenever you have a goal to reach, having an accountability partner will help you remember that there is someone else who is watching your every ERP move. An accountability partner can be your spouse, but it often works better if she or he is a trusted friend or extended family member.

Spousal relationships can be complex and it might be more difficult for your spouse to say no when you get tempted to take a spontaneous vacation to Jamaica. An accountability partner who's removed from your personal financial situation will be able to be more objective and help you say no to the unplanned vacation.

When picking an accountability partner, choose someone who is financially responsible, who has a thorough understanding of why you want to retire early, and someone who is independent enough to call you out on behaviors that will take you further away from your goal. Also, pick someone you admire, someone who you can learn from, and someone who is also good at money management.

Find a Mentor

A mentor is another valuable partner you can use to help you achieve your early retirement goal. A good mentor for you is someone who has already achieved what you want to achieve or is far ahead of you in achieving it. Your list of potential mentors should be people who are easily accessible to you. Consider people you know from work, from church or other social groups, or from networking groups in your area. As you narrow down your list of mentors, it's smart to choose one who has the following qualities:

- Pick a mentor who has proven herself as a financial success by her own money management actions. This type of person will be better able to give valuable advice for financial questions when you have them.
- Look for someone who has quality leadership skills when searching for a mentor. A good mentor is also a good leader.
- Choose a mentor who holds himself to a high level of ethical behavior. Trustworthy and honest are among the characteristics that should describe your mentor.

When seeking out a mentor, ask people if they want to mentor you. Not all successful people have the time or desire to be a mentor; however, in my experience most successful people look forward to sharing what they have learned in order to help others.

Using a Mentor

It's important to have a relationship with your mentor that involves giving as well as taking (knowledge) from them. Look for opportunities to help your mentor when she needs help. Treat her as you would treat a friend, with respect and gratitude. Be there for her when you can, and make sure to say "thank you" for her help.

Your mentor has a life outside of coaching you, and it's important for you not to take up too much of his time. Talk with potential mentors beforehand about what their available time is for meeting, make a regular schedule (once a week, once a month, etc.), and be respectful of it.

As a mentee, you're not there to teach but to learn. Be respectful of your mentor by listening carefully to what he has to say and by considering his advice carefully. If your mentor has achieved what you desire to achieve, it's likely he has a lot of valuable knowledge to share.

After you've "made it big" and achieved your ERP, don't forget the people who helped you get there. Keep in contact with them even after your mentor/mentee relationship has ended and continue to maintain the friendship if possible. Also, honor your mentor by being available to mentor someone who asks you.

Take Advantage of Continuing Education

Another way you can help stay motivated to stick with your ERP is to continually educate yourself on early retirement and money management/wealth growth. The more time you spend on educating yourself on building wealth and reducing expenses, the more information you will gather for making your plan happen. Studies show that 88 percent of wealthy people read nonfiction books or articles for thirty minutes or more each day. The financially successful practice continuing education because, as the old saying goes, knowledge equals power. If you want to continue to succeed with your ERP it's important to continue your financial education. Appendix D contains resources to enable you to do that.

If you are willing to be committed to continually learning from others whose beliefs align with your vision and who are further along than you in reaching financial freedom, you will find it easier to stick with your ERP.

Create or Join a Community of Like-Minded Individuals

Another way you can help yourself stay motivated to achieve your goals is to get involved with a community of people who have the same goals as you. That community can be in the form of an online forum or Facebook group, or in the form of a Mastermind group that meets in person at a brick-and-mortar location.

By networking both online and in person, you can find like-minded people with whom you can discuss and discover ways to increase your net worth and reach your ERP on time. Those groups and forums can be focused on financial independence, early retirement, real estate investing, business ownership, stock market investing, or all of the above.

Look for groups (or tailor your own) that discuss the topics that are relevant to you and your ERP, and use them as motivation to stay on track. Social media outlets and Google searches in your area will help you find groups to join. If you can't find one, use social media outlets to create your own group.

My Method and Why It Works

I believe in the information I've shared in this book because I've used it myself and it is working for me. My wife and I are free of consumer debt and will have paid off our mortgage in just a few short years. Although we are not technically financially independent yet, we are on track to be so by the time I am forty-two years old. At just forty-two years old I will have enough money in investments that I will be able to retire, should I choose to at that time.

Slow and Steady Wins the Race

Remember that slow and steady is the key to early retirement. When my wife and I started out with $52,000 in debt and a large mortgage, I never would have dreamed that we would achieve such results in such a short period. At the time, we were overwhelmed with how much debt we had and would have been happy just to be consumer debt–free. We sold my brand-new car, which was upside down, and that got rid of a car payment. We took the extra money from my former car payment and used it to pay down our debt. We sold anything we didn't need, and I even got a second job delivering pizzas to make some additional income. We did whatever we could to reduce our expenses as well, and within eighteen months all of that debt was gone!

By staying committed to working the plan even after our consumer debt was paid off, we've watched our wealth grow and our mortgage balance diminish at a surprisingly fast rate. We took the money we were paying toward consumer debt and used it as extra payments on the mortgage.

As you do the same, that snowball will start to roll downhill, and your net worth will increase at a faster rate as well.

Tried-and-True Strategies

Another reason our plan is working is that we are sticking with investment strategies that have proven true over the long term. We invest in the stock market with an appropriate risk balance for us, using primarily index funds, and I work my business to the best of my ability, using the skills that I have to help others. As we talked about earlier in this chapter, it's important to stick with proven strategies and avoid get-rich-quick schemes that will likely take you further away from your ERP goals.

Building true wealth requires consistency. The "fast path" to financial independence doesn't have a proven track record. While it may work for a select few, the failure rates for these paths are extremely high.

Don't risk your future—instead stick with proven methods for increasing net worth and be persistent in working your plan. Financial independence will come.

CHAPTER 9

How and When to Track Your Plan

"If you aim at nothing, you'll hit it every time."
—Zig Ziglar

We talked briefly about tracking your plan earlier on in the book. Now I want to expand on why it's so important to do this.

There's a popular quote about success that says "You only improve what you measure." When you are preparing for a race, you might record the distance you run each day and how fast you run it. When you are trying to lose weight you keep track of how many calories you eat each day.

For instance, let's say your goal is to lose ten pounds. To lose one pound you need to eat 3,500 less calories per week than what your body needs. Let's say your body needs 2,500 calories a day to maintain your current weight. That comes out to 17,500 calories per week. If you want to lose a pound a week, you'll have to reduce your weekly calorie intake to 14,000 calories. One way to help ensure you are eating the right amount of calories is to track caloric intake via a calorie tracking app or a notebook. By tracking what you eat each day and how many calories each item contains, you can help ensure you don't go over your target weekly calorie goal of 14,000 calories.

Likewise, when you're working to achieve early retirement, it's important to track your spending, use a budget, track your debt-to-income ratio, and track your net worth. The act of tracking your plan and working to keep motivated to stay with that plan is what will get you to early retirement.

As we talked about in Chapter 4, remembering the opportunity cost of items you are spending your money on will help you realign your spending and get a clearer focus on your financial goals. When you set a goal to lose weight, you set and track your plan with to-dos such as eating a salad for lunch instead of a burger and fries, and setting aside thirty minutes a day to exercise.

When you have a goal to retire early you need to make a plan and track it, working to lower expenses as you determine the opportunity cost of those expenses and finding ways to put more cash toward your ERP.

The Budget

Your budget is your monthly financial blueprint. It gives you a plan for how best to use the dollars you earn to reach your ERP goals. In practical terms, the budget is where you subtract your expenses from your income to figure out whether you have money left over, a surplus, or are in the negative, a deficit. Needless to say, the goal of a budget is to make sure that you have a surplus and not a deficit.

Track Spending

Tracking your spending can help you stick to your budget. You can use online software, a spreadsheet, or a smartphone app to help you see if your spending aligns with your budget. Expense tracking can also provide an at-a-glance assessment to call out areas in which you might be spending too much so that you can cut costs. If you find that you are overspending, especially in particular areas, then it is time to revisit your budget.

For instance, if you look at your budget and see that your entertainment expenses are too high, you can immediately reduce your entertainment spending and funnel more money toward your ERP. You can even cut spending on entertainment altogether and instead use free entertainment such as movie nights or game nights at home. Or you can figure out ways to do the activities you love without spending so much money on them. If you like to see movies at the theater you can go during matinees instead of seeing evening shows, or you can subscribe to services such as Netflix and Hulu. If you like to dine out, you can use two-for-one meal promotion coupons, eat appetizers during happy hour specials, or go out for lunch instead of dinner, as most restaurants have cheaper prices during lunch.

If you are spending too much on meals you can cut back by taking lunch to work from home instead of eating out daily or make coffee from home instead of purchasing it from the local coffee shop. If you are seeing big spending numbers in your clothing purchases you can start shopping at consignment stores or stop buying new clothes except when you really need them. If you are spending too much on salon and self-care expenses such as gym memberships you can reduce expenditures by going to a less expensive salon, going less frequently, or choosing to work out at home instead of at the gym.

The intent of tracking your spending is to give you a clear picture of where your money is going, to find out if it's different from the expenses spelled out in your budget. With that information at your fingertips, you can recognize any spending that leads to lost opportunities (such as additional funding for your ERP) and a longer path to financial independence and remedy it sooner instead of later.

If you are not tracking your spending, you run the risk of spending money without realizing it. Without a tracking system it is too easy to spend money and forget that you ever spent it. You'll think that you spent $100 on eating out when in reality you likely spent $200. Life is just too busy for you to keep track of every dime you spend without a little help.

A spend-tracking plan will help you to see in black and white exactly how much you are spending each month and what you are spending it on, so that you can avoid the black hole of "where does my money go?" and make sure you are spending your money intentionally and minimizing waste. When you can see leaks in your spending, you'll find it hard to ignore the lost opportunity cost and easier to make changes in your spending habits as you're faced with the clear truth about what you are spending your money on.

Knowing Your Debt-to-Income Ratio

Knowing your debt-to-income ratio (DTI—your total monthly debt payments divided by your total monthly gross income) will help ensure you are making progress toward the DTI goal you've set for the purposes of early retirement. Knowing your debt-to-income ratio will give you a good indication of how financially stable you are. The lower your DTI, the more flexibility you'll have to reduce spending before and after retirement, which can help lower your target ERP number. It may help you to check your DTI on a quarterly basis, keeping track of it on a spreadsheet so that you can be sure your DTI is headed in the right direction: downward.

Tracking Your Net Worth

Your net worth, the true value of what you own, is the big picture number of how you are doing on your ERP. To calculate net worth, you need to know your total assets (what you have) and your total liabilities (what you owe); the difference between the two equals your net worth. Experts suggest tracking your net worth in two ways: including liquid and nonliquid assets, and then tracking using liquid assets only.

Nonliquid assets can't be converted quickly into cash and include any homes you own, rental properties, retirement accounts (such as 401(k)s and IRA accounts), and larger material items such as cars, boats, fine jewelry, etc. Liquid assets include any cash you have in bank savings, checking, and money market accounts and any nonretirement investment accounts with holdings you could sell today and get cash for.

Tracking your net worth using your liquid assets only gives you an idea of how much cash you could access quickly if need be. Tracking your net worth using all assets gives you a better big-picture view of how you are doing in terms of reaching your early retirement goals.

Net worth tracking is a point of measure that financial experts use to determine the financial solvency and stability of a person. For instance, every year *Forbes* magazine puts out a list of the four hundred wealthiest people in America. This year the minimum entry-level net worth to make this elite list of the country's wealthiest people was $1.7 billion. In order to see who qualifies to make the list, *Forbes* measures potential competitors' net worth.

People with substantial net worth tend to focus on acquiring appreciating assets (assets that go up in value). Increasing net worth and prioritizing appreciating assets over depreciating ones (cars, electronics, and basic consumer goods) helps people become and stay rich.

If you are going to achieve your goal of building enough wealth so that you can retire early, make building your net worth a higher priority than obtaining instant gratification purchases that will diminish your wealth instead of increase it.

The Power in Assessing Your Progress

Assessing your progress gives you power. It gives you the power to spot hidden hindrances in your ERP and the power to spot potential for improvement. If you are continually tracking each area of your plan, you can make changes to your plan when needed and avoid months of financial loss that could hinder your plan.

How to Measure Your Progress

The first step in tracking the progress in your plan is to make a schedule that sets benchmarks as you go. It's important that your benchmarks are realistic yet challenging. Your benchmarks need to stretch your ability to save without being so far-reaching that they will be impossible to achieve or hinder your ability to cover basic needs.

Setting the Right Benchmarks

It's helpful to set benchmarks for your ERP and to make sure your benchmarks are realistic for your income and current situation. For instance, if your final ERP number is $1 million and you're starting at zero, it might not be realistic to reach $250,000 in your first year.

When runners set a goal of running a marathon, they keep in mind the goal of being able to run the entire 26.2-mile stretch, but they also set aside that goal and focus on reaching a predetermined set of benchmarks that will eventually lead to their goal of running the marathon.

Instead of working just to be able to run farther, they work on increased physical and mental fitness. Running long distances is just as much a mental game as it is a physical one. When you run long distances, the first leg of your journey—whether it's two miles or twenty miles—is often tedious. Then your body gets into a groove and the middle section of the run is easier. When you come to the last section of your run, things start to get tough again and your mind starts to try to convince you to quit. *You've already run so far. You're doing better than most people. Most people never leave the couch, but you've run three times this week. It's okay to give up. Running eight miles instead of the ten you set out to run is great. You can do more tomorrow.* These are the messages your mind starts telling you as you hit that last leg of your run.

Mini-Goals

When runners set benchmarks for running a long distance such as a marathon or half-marathon, they start by conditioning their body. They set slow and methodic goals for increasing their pace as well as their distance. Instead of pushing themselves too much, they go for mini-goals that will stretch their physical ability without pushing themselves to the point of exhaustion.

In the same way they work on mental conditioning. They replace "You've done so well already—it's okay to quit" messages with "You've got this—you can do it" messages. They keep in mind the end goal of completing the entire marathon, but they give more focus to the smaller goals that will eventually help them achieve the physical and mental fitness they need to be able to complete the run.

Because runners are making their main focus the little goals that help them make small advances in their fitness level, they don't get overwhelmed at the thought of the big goal. Those smaller benchmark goals are easier to reach so it doesn't seem like such a big deal; however, those small goals tackled one right after the other will eventually lead to the ability to complete the entire marathon.

In the same way, financial benchmarks will help you stay on track to get to the point where you've got enough saved and invested so that you can retire early as long as you set small achievable benchmarks on the road to your big goal of financial independence.

For example, your first benchmark might be to reduce spending on "wants" by $100 the first month to bring you closer to staying on budget. Your next benchmark might be to have a $200 budget surplus. Once you hit that measure, you'll know that your budget is working for you. Once you're in the habit of sticking to your budget, you can start setting ERP benchmarks to help build up your savings. Each benchmark you meet will show you that you're well on the way to the end goal of early retirement.

Being Realistic with Benchmarks

As you prepare to set your benchmarks, it's wise to take into account your annual income, the amount of debt you may need to pay off, and your path for wealth growth. Expecting a 25 percent return on the stock market in a single year isn't a realistic benchmark; however, expecting a 25 percent return in a year via real estate investing could be realistic—if housing prices are on the rise. If you buy a house at a great deal and do any needed improvements yourself, selling that house for that kind of profit could be possible.

In the same way, paying off $100,000 in debt in one year when your income is only $75,000 isn't a realistic benchmark for debt reduction. However, if you're planning on selling one or more large-ticket items in order to reduce debt, paying off $100,000 in debt in a year could happen. For instance, if you trade in a paid-off car that's worth $20,000 for a $5,000 car, you can put the remaining $15,000 toward debt. Or if you sell your house and downsize to one that is worth half the value, you could have tens of thousands of dollars to put toward debt payoff. This is what I mean by setting realistic benchmarks for reaching your plan's goals.

Setting achievable benchmarks that still challenge your budget will help encourage you to keep moving toward the early retirement numbers you've set in place.

Quantify Your Goals

Quantifying your ERP goals is another way to track your progress. To quantify something is to put it in numbers. When you quantify your ERP end goal, you are determining the exact number of dollars you need in your investment account in order to retire.

One way to determine what you need to retire is to consider the Multiply by Twenty-Five Rule. The basic theory behind this rule is that you need twenty-five times your postretirement desired annual income in your investment account before you can retire. So, if you want $50,000 per year in postretirement income, your investment account needs to have $1,250,000 in it.

As we discussed earlier in this book, before you decide how much money you need to live on each year postretirement, you'll want to think about several things. First, what type of postretirement lifestyle do you plan on living? Do you plan on keeping your expenses relatively basic, or will there be golf club memberships, extensive travel, and other costly hobbies?

It's also wise to factor in inflation. So, during your first year you might pull out 4 percent, but during your second year you might need to pull out 4.03 percent from your investment account in order to cover inflation. Although such a small increase in withdrawals may seem irrelevant, it will add up over time and affect how long your retirement income lasts.

The Multiply by Twenty-Five Rule works together with the 4 percent withdrawal rule (where you withdraw 4 percent of your original retirement account balance every year). However, it is important to consider some further things if you're using the 4 percent rule (or the Multiply by Twenty-Five Rule) to determine your ERP number.

First, the Multiply by Twenty-Five Rule is based on getting at least 4 percent annual returns, which calls for a high proportion of stocks in your investment account. If your investment account holds low-risk assets, which typically come with lower returns, a 4 percent withdrawal rate could be too high. Second, large market downturns—especially if they occur during the first few years of retirement—could seriously affect your postretirement income, both by reducing your account balance and the returns you would have made on the balance you lost. Third, the Twenty-Five Rule does not factor in taxes, which could affect your income based on how much you are pulling out of your investment accounts each year.

As I mentioned earlier in the book, a safer way to quantify your ERP's end number would be to plan on a 3.5 percent withdrawal rate instead of 4 percent. That would change the amount of money you need to retire (you'd need less since the number you need to live on each year would be a lesser percentage of your total) but it would give you an added cushion that might provide more peace of mind as you retire early.

Consider Additional Income

Another thing to consider when quantifying your ERP end goal is that the Multiply by Twenty-Five Rule doesn't include additional income. If you plan on working part-time or at a freelancing job, or if you'll eventually have pension benefits or other money such as Social Security coming in monthly, this extra money will give you a cushion and decrease the amount you'll need to withdraw from your investment account each month. These are all factors to consider when quantifying your ERP target number.

It's also a smart idea to consider quantifying the mini-goals that lead up to your ERP goal as well. Other goals you can quantify as you work your way toward early retirement include your budget goals (how much of your monthly income are you saving toward your ERP and can/should you increase that number?), your debt-reduction goals (in how many years do you want each debt paid off?), and your asset increase or reduction goals (where will you live, what will you own, where will you store the assets, and how will you pay to store and maintain those assets?).

By quantifying your end ERP goal and the mini-goals that you want to achieve along the way, you'll have solid benchmarks that will help you determine if you're on track with your early retirement plan.

How Often Should You Assess Progress?

The answer to this question may vary from person to person, but there are some basic rules you can use as a starting point for monitoring progress on your ERP. Monitoring your progress on a regular basis, as well as checking in on progress and any adjustments that need to be made after a major event such as a job loss, will help you revise your plan before it gets seriously off track.

Monthly, Semiannual, and Annual Checks

Your budget and spend-tracking sheet will help you determine every month whether or not your plan is on track. These are "quick glance" tools that can be helpful in ensuring that you are doing what you planned to do regarding achieving your ERP goals.

Depending on your personality, it can be helpful to do a larger-scale check on your ERP either annually or semiannually. For this check you'll want to assess stock market performance and make decisions about whether to reallocate your investment dollars, and check to be sure that your annual savings and profit numbers are still in line with your end ERP goal. It's also a good time to check on (hopefully positive) changes in your net worth and your DTI; you'll want to make sure both are moving in the right direction. With that information, you'll be able to decide whether big changes to your plan are needed and how you'll implement those changes. You may need to increase your income, push back your ERP date, or even move your ERP date up a year or two in the case that progress is occurring faster than you expected.

Major Life Events

The occurrence of a major life event is another time to check your ERP plan and see if it needs to be modified. An unexpected job change (or even an expected job change) might affect your ERP goals—either for the better or for the worse. A new baby can change your goals, as it will take more of your income to raise an additional child; a child moving out or graduating from college will have the opposite effect.

A decision to move to another state, to marry (or divorce), or other major life events will likely have an effect on your ERP, and your plan should be reassessed at times when major life events such as these occur.

There's an old saying about goals: "The closer you track it, the more likely you are to attain it." While this is true, it's important not to spend too much time tracking your plan either. Obsessing over your ERP numbers every week or stressing out at every market downturn won't help you reach your goals. Instead, it will likely induce fear that may cause you to make quick decisions that could affect your plans adversely. As you work toward early retirement, consider tracking your progress regularly but not obsessively.

Keep It Simple with Software

Aside from your basic computer spreadsheet, there are online software programs and other financial apps that can help you track your progress. The number of financial apps, financial software such as Quicken, and cloud-based financial tracking programs can be overwhelming. We'll talk about some of the best here, including two of my favorites: Mint and Personal Capital.

Mint

Mint is a website that focuses on budgeting to help you reach your financial goals. With Mint you can create a budget, track and pay bills, and see at a glance your spending by category. Mint also tracks your investments, but its main goal is to help you budget well.

Mint gives you a picture of how much you owe and to whom, breaks down all of your spending by category, and allows both you and your spouse access to every money transaction so there's no miscommunication about how much cash is available.

Users can even rename and add spending categories. The app also lets you know when payments are coming due or what the daily balance in your account is so that you can have enough notice to avoid being charged late fees by creditors or overdraft/below-minimum balance fees by your bank.

An additional bonus feature is that Mint notifies you right away if it sees a large or unusual purchase that is different from your usual activity.

Mint is a free service (so you will have to tolerate ads) and can't actually do anything to your money unless you use their automated bill-paying service. The bill-paying service is free if you use your bank account, but transaction fees do apply if you pay bills using a credit card or Mint's Express Pay feature.

Personal Capital

Personal Capital is more investment-focused than Mint. Although it does have the capability to help you create a budget and track your spending (and it does these things well), Personal Capital's main goal is to help you grow your wealth via investing. It offers both automated investing advice based on your risk tolerance information and professional real-person advice from financial advisers.

Along with tracking your net worth, Personal Capital allows you to see all of your investment accounts in one place. It also provides extra services such as its 401(k) and investment fee analyzer that helps you have full transparency for all fees you are being charged for investing.

Personal Capital also helps you analyze if you are on track to have enough money for retirement and how other expenses such as kids' college costs will affect your ability to retire. It's a comprehensive service that over a million users utilize to help them manage their money in a way that is conducive to increasing their net worth. Personal Capital doesn't charge anything for budgeting and spend-tracking, and has minimal fees for investment management, starting at 0.89 percent per year and going down as your net worth increases.

Tiller

Tiller is a spreadsheet-based budgeting app that allows you to get daily feeds from your financial institution and create up to five different spreadsheets for tracking both business and personal expenses. You control who has access to the spreadsheets, which means you can share them with your spouse, your kids, your accountant, or anyone else who needs to have access to your financial transactions or expenses. Tiller also sends daily emails updating you on your current financial picture so that you always know where you are financially. At $5 a month (the first thirty days are free, and you won't have to tolerate ads) Tiller is affordable too.

You Need a Budget

You Need a Budget (YNAB) works a bit differently. Along with keeping track of your spending and account balances, YNAB has the capability to help you set goals for saving money and paying off debt and gives you tips for achieving those goals. It also gives you estimated dates for reaching those goals based on your current spending and helps you construct spending scenarios that will help you reach your financial goals faster. YNAB is free for the first thirty-four days and costs only $50 per year after that. Like the other financial tracking apps and services we've mentioned here, YNAB is secure and has high-level encryption to keep your information safe.

A personal finance software or cloud-based program will help you track your progress in a way that ensures you stay on target for your ERP goals. It's important when choosing which tracking program you'll use that you pay special attention to security.

Having your information online at a cloud-based site does involve some risk, but quality companies such as Personal Capital and Mint have extensively encrypted security programs in place to ensure your private information stays private. When researching online financial software options, be sure to research security levels for each company you're considering as well.

Investment Fees

One thing that's important to track is fees. The impact that investment fees can have on a portfolio is shown in the following chart.

The investor started his investment account with $25,000 at age twenty-five. He invested an additional $10,000 a year for forty years and earned an average 7 percent return. Here's how much money his 1.02 percent expense ratio cost him.

Number of Years Invested	Portfolio Value Lost to Fees	After-Fee Investment Value	Value Lost to Fees
10	$11,343	$166,000	6.4%
20	$61,696	$435,001	12.4%
30	$210,700	$914,215	18.7%
40	$592,798	$1.77 million	25.1%

(Source: www.nerdwallet.com/blog/investing/millennial-retirement-fees-one-percent-half-million-savings-impact/)

Over the course of time, fees can indeed have a serious impact on your investment portfolio, and that's why it's important as you track your plan that you track the fees you pay as well.

Tracking your plan in a smart and secure manner will help you reach your early retirement goals within your desired time frame. Start working on the type of tracking system that's best for you and your spouse, and begin implementing it or modifying it today as needed.

CHAPTER 10

How to Deal with Setbacks

Life is not perfect and things don't always go as expected. Nearly every plan comes with detours and setbacks. Your ERP will overcome any setbacks faster if you anticipate them ahead of time and build in safeguards for handling them. In this chapter we'll talk about potential setbacks that could hinder your plan and some of the stopgaps you can put in place to help overcome those setbacks.

Fallout from Economic Downturn

Economic downturns can affect any of the three avenues you choose for funding your ERP, whether that be real estate, the stock market, or business ownership. For instance, although the long-term history of the stock market has proven positive returns, there have been—and will always be—a few slumps and crashes along the way. During the 1929 crash the stock market lost 50 percent of its value. During the 1987 crash it lost nearly 23 percent. And during the 2008 crash the market lost more than 30 percent of its value. Keep in mind that these statistics speak to the market as a whole; individual stocks, industries, and sectors can fare much worse.

Stock market investors aren't the only ones affected by economic downturns. Those investing in business ownership might suffer from sales slumps, and real estate investors could be hurt by declining property values. These are just a few of the ways an economic downturn could negatively affect your ERP. Realizing that, and putting safeguards in place, can help you better weather these potential setbacks.

An Emergency Fund

As we've talked about throughout the book, building an emergency fund is essential to a well-thought-out ERP. Your emergency fund should contain a minimum of three months' worth of expenses; ideally, it should hold enough to cover six months' worth of expenses. If you know that an impending setback—such as a job layoff or a change in your family situation—is on the horizon, I would suggest a twelve-month emergency fund as a buffer to ensure you have the money to weather life changes or economic downturns with minimal impact on your ERP.

Insurance

Insurance can also be a smart investment for helping you cover setbacks. Medical, dental, homeowners, life, and disability insurance options should be investigated to help you determine how you can best protect your family and your ERP from some type of unexpected event. Insurance policies can help you cover costs that you would otherwise have to pay out of pocket. Disability insurance will pay you what you would earn at your job if you couldn't work for some physical or psychological reason. Homeowners insurance will cover incidents including damage to your house, minimizing your out-of-pocket cost for large repairs such as damage caused by storms and theft losses. Umbrella policies are becoming increasingly common among the wealthy as they provide coverage of $1 million or more toward a large variety of potential disasters.

Portfolio Loss

As I said, economic downturn could mean large losses in your investment portfolio. However, it is important to keep a long-term perspective when it comes to investing in the stock market. A loss is only final if you sell your investment. If you've chosen solid investments for their long-term prospects, there's a very good chance those could rebound from recession, so holding on to them may allow your ERP to regain its lost value—and even prosper. In fact, many people who lost money during the 2008 recession but held on to their shares have regained their pre-crash portfolio values and have watched them grow even bigger.

While stock market losses can have an impact on your ERP, if you stay with your plan and ride out the waves in the market your investments will probably rise again, as long as they have enough recovery time. To help ensure that, pay attention to your asset allocation. Whereas you might have a 70/30 stock versus bond allocation when you're in your thirties, consider revising that allocation every ten years or so, reducing the risk level of your portfolio as you get closer to your personal retirement age.

Job Loss

Negative changes in the economy could have a direct impact on your job security as companies cut expenses or even go out of business. The thing to remember about job layoffs is that although you can't control the event, you can control the outcome.

It's easy to get discouraged when experiencing a job layoff and take it as a personal assault on your character. Instead of viewing a job loss as a negative thing or as a direct reflection on your value as a person, view it as an opportunity. Use a layoff as a chance to do self-analysis of your work ethic and your personal skills. If the layoff was a result of poor performance or a lack of necessary skills, set a plan in place to improve in those areas. If that wasn't the case, remind yourself that you are a valuable employee, that business is business, and just move on.

No matter what the reason for the event, a job layoff is a great opportunity to reevaluate your career. Did you like what you were doing at work? Is there something else you'd rather do? Can you make more money at another company or in another type of job? Use your layoff as a chance to improve your work situation so that the working years that lead up to the fulfillment of your ERP are happy ones. Take the opportunity to improve your working life and your personal life and pursue a career position that is better than the one you lost.

Real Estate Devaluation

If you've chosen real estate as your path to financial independence, a real estate crash can have an impact on your ERP. However, it's important to remember that using rental real estate for your ERP is all about cash flow. It's about the money your properties bring in each month and not so much about the value of the property itself.

That said, changes in the real estate market could have an impact on your vacancy rate, so it's wise to consider building in a cushion when you purchase your property. You can do that by putting as much down on the property as possible when you buy it (or better yet, buy it with cash) and by having a substantial emergency fund set aside for your rental properties that will help cover vacancy periods.

A Changing Family

A change in your family situation might call for a change in your ERP benchmarks. A marriage, divorce, or new children joining your family will change your financial situation, and you'll need to reevaluate your early retirement plan. As your family dynamics change—especially when it applies to raising additional kids—it's important to count the costs ahead of time so that you can work the additional costs into your budget and ERP.

Adding Children

Costs for additional children will be different for everyone depending on lifestyle. You may have daycare costs or you may not. You might buy gently used clothing at garage sales for your new child, or you might prefer name-brand clothes. Determine how a changing family will change your financial needs and rework your budget to reflect the additional costs and the potential changes to your ERP goals. When considering adding another child to your family, it's important to make a list of all potential costs and how you will cover them without negatively affecting your ERP. For instance, will both spouses still wish to work if another child is added? How will you pay for daycare costs or cover the lost income if one parent decides to stay home? How will out-of-pocket medical costs for the birth of the child be paid? What do you expect to spend on early care costs such as diapers and formula? How will you pay for the increase in food costs? Orthodontia care? What will you contribute toward the child's college education? The more prepared you are for the many costs of adding an additional child to your family, the less impact the expenses for that child will have on your ERP.

Caring for Aging Parents

Having to care for aging parents may also affect your early retirement plan. You can help minimize the impact this has on your ERP by talking with your parents now about their preparations for getting older. Ask them if they have a plan to cover the many different stages of growing old. Do they have long-term care coverage? What is their debt and savings situation? Where do they plan to live as they get older? What are their plans, and how are they prepared financially for the possibility of needing assisted living?

Encourage and assist your parents to formulate a plan that protects them and their children (including you) financially as well. Determine ahead of time who will care for your parents as they age and how their needs can be met both physically and financially in a way that works for the entire family.

If too much time has passed and the care of your aging parents is left on your shoulders, you will need to work the additional expenses into your budget and ERP just as you would any other expense. Readjust the numbers in a way that allows you to reach your early retirement goals even if it may take longer than originally expected. For instance, where will your aging parents live and who will cover the cost-of-living expenses? If your parents don't have substantial assets, government assistance may cover many expenses such as assisted living. If your parents don't qualify for government assistance, their assets will need to be used to cover care expenses. Determine how much the type of care they need costs and how quickly those costs will diminish your parents' assets. Or, if you decide your aging parents will live with you, determine costs of in-home care that may be necessary. Take into account the monthly cost for any prescription medication needed as well as any other medical and dental care. Dentures, hearing aids, and other accessibility items such as wheelchairs should all be accounted for as you figure out how much caring for aging parents may cost you.

Adult Children Moving Back Home

Sometimes adult children want or need to move back home. Only you can decide whether or not an adult child moving back home will affect your ERP. It's helpful to ask some questions and set boundaries before you agree to let your adult child move home so everyone knows what is expected.

Why is your child moving back home? How long does she or he plan to live there? What type of contributions will your offspring be making to the family during the stay at home? How much rent will you charge? What chores and household help will they be responsible for? Sometimes adult kids need to move back home and that's okay. As a parent, your job is to make sure that a move back home will help your child and not enable him or her to live a less-than-responsible life.

For instance, it might be a good idea to set a time limit. Also, ensure that your child is doing what he needs to do to become independent again, whether that means finishing up college or working at a job that will help correct any potential financial problems. If your child's reason for returning home involves physical or emotional problems, do what you can to help him get the medical care he needs so he can return to an independent life.

Setting clear rules is also a good idea when allowing adult children to move back home. Be sure your child has responsibilities for helping around the house and consider charging rent if it is appropriate. A move back home shouldn't be an opportunity for an adult child to avoid living a responsible life, but instead a pathway to return to an independent life.

If your adult child needs to move home and is not physically or emotionally able to return to an independent life, it will be necessary to make the appropriate changes to your ERP to account for the additional long-term expenses. You'll need to determine what medical expenses your adult child needs and who will cover those costs. For instance, is there insurance or government assistance available to help your child cover costs? If not, is your child eligible to participate in your insurance or healthcare sharing plan? How will you pay for out-of-pocket costs such as deductibles for doctor's visits and medications? Any time there are additional unexpected expenses, those costs must be added into your budget and assessed for how they will affect your ERP both before and after you retire.

Caring for Grandchildren

You may need to reevaluate your ERP in several different ways if you want to help care for your grandchildren. For instance, if you or your spouse have decided to care for your grandchildren while your adult child works, that may decrease your income potential, a factor that needs to be taken into consideration regarding your early retirement plan.

You might also find yourself in a situation where you need to consider the possibility of raising your grandchildren because your adult child can't or won't. Nearly 3 million grandparents are raising grandchildren in today's society.

If you find yourself in a situation where raising your grandkids is inevitable, you'll have to rework your budget and work the additional expenses into your early retirement plan. Recalculate your budget with your new added expenses and reset the benchmarks and goals needed to obtain your ERP goal. Having to raise grandkids doesn't necessarily mean early retirement is out of the picture. Many times states provide income help for those raising grandkids on a permanent basis. Or, you may need to change your idea of what retirement looks like. If your original ERP included an abundance of travel, those travel expenses may need to be replaced with child-rearing costs. It's all about prioritization and planning.

Medical Issues

Major illness, chronic illness, and injury do happen. Some of these things are in your control and some of them aren't. Taking good care of your health can play a major part in avoiding medical issues that could affect your early retirement goals. Eating well, exercising, driving safely, and minimizing exposure to dangerous activities may help you avoid many illnesses or injuries that could cause a setback to your ERP.

Major medical issues can have a substantial impact on your ability to retire early. Ongoing medical costs can easily run into the six digits. The goal as you plan to minimize that impact should be to control what you can and plan for what you can't.

An emergency fund and the right insurance coverage will help you to plan financially for medical illnesses and injuries you can't control. Depending on your individual situation, short- and long-term disability insurance might be a wise investment. In my case, my business helps companies improve search engine optimization rankings. I could do my job even if I had an injury to my arms and legs. Because I could do my job with limited mobility I don't carry disability insurance. However, if a person doing my type of work suffered a traumatic brain injury he could no longer do his job, and disability insurance would be a tremendous help. If you're not sure whether disability insurance makes sense for you, talk with someone (not someone selling insurance) about which types of insurance policies could be most beneficial for you and about how potential medical conditions could affect your ability to do your job.

Long-Term Care Insurance

Many financial professionals consider long-term care insurance a must. As an early retiree, your chances of needing long-term care are minimal, but as you age the chance of needing long-term care increases. It's important when creating your ERP that you consider not just your younger retired years, but your older retired years as well. Planning in advance for how you will cover long-term care costs via insurance will help you avoid financial troubles that could arise if you don't address long-term care needs until you are older.

Identity Theft

Identity theft is not only an inconvenience, it can have a major impact on your financial assets, your debt, and your credit rating. According to the Department of Justice the total cash losses stemming from identity theft in 2014 were $15.4 billion. Identity thieves are continually coming up with new ways to steal money from unsuspecting people and businesses.

There are ways you can protect yourself and your family from identity theft. First, you can start by keeping a close eye on your finances and your credit report. Keep regular track of your bank and credit accounts to ensure the balances and transactions are in line with your personal purchases. AnnualCreditReport.com allows people to check all three of their personal credit bureau reports once a year at no charge. You're also entitled to a free copy of your credit report if the report is wrong due to fraud—including identity theft. By checking your credit report regularly you can identify potential fraudulent activity early.

Second, you can help protect yourself from identity theft by safe-guarding your personal and financial information. Following are some ideas for safeguarding your information from potential identity theft.

Be Careful about Giving Out Personal Information

Being choosy about how and where you share personal information will help you protect your identity. Don't give out your personal in-formation to anyone who doesn't truly need it. Many businesses want to have information such as your social security number or credit card number on file, but they don't truly need this information to serve you as a customer.

Don't Respond to Unsolicited Requests for Your Personal Information

Phone calls or emails requesting personal information such as your social security number, your birthdate, your address, or your credit card numbers could be part of attempts to steal your identity. In most cases, those contacts are initiated by identity thieves; banks, govern-ment agencies, and reputable businesses will not contact you by phone or email to request that information. If you do get such a phone call or email, and you think it might be legit, verify it independently by checking the call-back number or website address.

Install Reputable Antivirus Software and Firewalls on Your Home Computer

Install quality antivirus software on your computer, update it regu-larly, and run frequent scans to check for potential viruses and malware that could be working to steal your private information. Remember, though, that these programs are responding to threats that already exist; they can't protect you from malicious software that hasn't been detected yet. I use one called AVG and the best part is that it is free. Check websites such as PCMag.com for reviews on antivirus software so that you can research the best in current antivirus software.

Create Complex Passwords and Store Them Safely

The account passwords you create should contain a variety of numbers, letters, and symbols that would make it difficult for identity thieves to uncover. Store those passwords in a safe place at home and in one other safe place. Change the passwords on your most sensitive accounts—bank, investment, and medical—at least three times a year. And always change your password if a company you do business with has had its accounts breached.

Be Safe with Your Snail Mail

Identity thieves often check mailboxes and trash bins looking for personal information. Be sure to collect your mail daily, shred any mail that contains your personal information, and ask the post office to stop delivery of your mail if you are going to be away from home for more than a day or two. It's especially important to shred credit card offers; identity thieves can use these to secure credit in your name.

Monitor Your Credit

Checking your credit report regularly, in addition to getting your free annual credit report, can be a major deterrent to identity thieves. Companies such as Credit Karma and Credit Sesame have programs in place that will monitor your credit on a regular basis and notify you immediately if there is a suspected breach in the security of your information. These types of companies also have the capability to act quickly to stop an identity thief from further damaging your finances.

If you aren't signed up with a service and you find a potential security breach on your credit report, call the individual creditor and all three credit bureau reporting agencies immediately to notify them of the potential fraudulent activity. Here is the contact information for the three major credit bureaus:

- **Experian:** 1-888-397-3742; www.experian.com
- **Equifax:** 1-866-349-5191; www.equifax.com
- **TransUnion:** 1-877-322-8228; www.transunion.com

Any steps you take to avoid identity theft are good ones and will help keep your finances and your credit record from suffering financial and other loss, and will help you protect your ERP goals at the same time.

Keep Your *Why* in Front of You

Any setbacks you experience can be overcome financially with the help of a good plan and psychologically by remembering your *why*. When you first decided that you wanted to retire early, you had a vision that helped you create a plan and gave you the drive to achieve that plan. Returning to that vision and the *why* behind it will motivate you to persevere through any setbacks that occur.

Why the Grass Is Greener after Early Retirement

The whole reason you—and thousands of other people—are drawn to the idea of early retirement is because it provides freedom. Somewhere along the way you decided you wanted more than to work every day until you're sixty-five.

The idea of the financial freedom that allows you to have choices about where you live and work appealed to you. Early retirement gives people the option to live an independent life. They can live where they want to live without being tied to the schedule of an employer.

Likely the greatest gift early retirement can give you is time. When you are no longer stuck working a typical job you have more time to spend with the people you love, to pursue hobbies and interests that appeal to you, and to make a difference in the world. You can fly to a foreign country for a charity trip on a whim or take your family to Italy for spring break—choices that aren't easily available for those living paycheck-to-paycheck and stuck in a traditional job.

Once you've accrued enough in investments and income to retire early, you have the choice to keep working as long as you want—or the choice to turn in your resignation letter and pursue any number of other choices.

If you follow through on your early retirement plan, you'll have the opportunity to do things and live life in a way that very few have, simply because you've chosen to use the money you earn in your working years in a way that produces a financially secure future. The gift of time alone is enough to convince most people to stick with their ERP through thick and thin. However, early retirement can come with negative side effects that most people don't think about until it's too late.

What They Don't Tell You about Early Retirement

Retiring early can have a downside that very few financially independent people talk about: a lack of purpose. This is possibly the most important part of this book. You began reading thinking you have the answer to a happy life and that the answer is financial independence and the ability to retire early. Then when you get there you're completely bored and totally let down.

You spend your days wasting way too much time browsing the Internet or watching stupid stuff on television. The excitement you had as you worked your plan is gone, you've had your fill of travel and living without limits for the year, and now you're just plain bored.

This happens to many people once they attain financial freedom. It happens because money is not the greatest achievement in life—purpose is. Without a purpose in life—a reason for living—you cannot obtain long-term happiness.

This is why it's vitally important that when you are creating your ERP you are not retiring away from something, but toward something else. Your reason for wanting to retire early and have the financial ability to do what you want has to include a vision and a purpose for your future.

Discovering what your early retirement purpose is now is of the utmost importance. What contributions do you want to make to the world? What community service causes or humanitarian projects can you get involved in that will give you a sense of purpose in life? One of the ways I help give my life purpose now is that I volunteer with an organization called Hustle PHX, a nonprofit that helps equip people in the inner city who want to become entrepreneurs by connecting them with mentors who can give them a real-life look into what it takes to start and run their own business. For the mentors like me, it offers a chance to pass on the knowledge learned through personal business ventures.

The number of opportunities to help make the world a better place truly is endless, and if you're going to avoid the boredom and unhappiness that can come with early retirement, now is the time to create your plan for what you will do with your days after you retire.

Making Life after Early Retirement All It's Meant to Be

Avoiding letdown and boredom after you reach early retirement starts with getting a vision of where you're going. Now—long before you've achieved your ERP—is the time to do that. Start by spending some time taking a serious look at the things that matter most to you. Get a vision of how you can best utilize your talents to help others. What issues matter to you? Write down a list of four or five humanitarian or community service missions that are important to you.

This may take some time and research, especially if you haven't been involved in a lot of charities or mentorship programs up until this point. If you don't know where to start, begin by identifying groups that you have compassion for.

Once you've made your list of four or five causes that are important to you, start doing some Internet research on how you can be involved in helping with those causes. If you love working with animals, Google an animal shelter or animal rehabilitation center in your area. If you like the thought of mentoring inner-city kids, Google "mentoring programs for kids" along with your city or state.

You may have to visit and volunteer with several different organizations before you find the one or two that fit you, and that's okay. The experience alone of visiting and volunteering with different organizations will help you determine and define what it is you really want to do with your time after early retirement.

Quarterly Check-Ins

Once your postretirement plan is in place, keep up with regular check-ins. Once you have achieved your ERP goals and are living a life in early retirement, quarterly check-ins are still a good idea. Quarterly assessment of your finances is important to make sure you're not withdrawing money at too fast a pace. Those check-ins will also help you be able to plan more easily for any unexpected expenses or life changes. If expenses suddenly increase due to an unexpected postretirement event such as the birth of another child, you'll need to reassess your expenses as well as your investment balances. If an unexpected change in expenses or decrease in your cash flow happens, you may need to revise your plan by getting part-time work to supplement your income or finding another way to increase funds so that your early retirement monies don't run out. Regular check-ins will keep you aware of your financial situation at all times so that shortfalls in income or increases in expenses can be handled in a timely manner, before things get out of hand.

Likewise, quarterly assessments of what is working and what's not working in your postretirement schedule will help you avoid burnout and disappointment.

Just like with your ERP, postretirement schedule modifications are okay and necessary. Not having enough to do will drain you of energy, and having too much on your schedule will leave you exhausted. It's important to find a balance, which may only come after several months of evaluations and modifications. Don't worry so much about arriving at the perfect retirement schedule; enjoy the journey that helps you get there.

Your ERP plan includes a serious focus on yourself, your money, and your goals. Your whole purpose is to create a life that fits your desires and it will likely take several years if not a decade or two to get "there."

It may come as a surprise then when you realize that early retirement isn't really about you at all. When most people start thinking about early retirement their thoughts are very "me" focused, but after you retire you'll soon find that serving yourself gets boring real fast. It's then that you find out that the real reason for early retirement is so you can have the freedom to make a difference in the lives of others. Instead of being driven so you can have the freedom to play all day, you'll be driven to figure out how you can use your gifts, talents, and knowledge to make a difference in the world.

As you learn to fulfill your purpose in early retirement, you'll come to realize that early retirement is more exciting than you ever could have imagined, not because you have the financial means and the time to do whatever you want, but because you have the financial means and the time to make a meaningful impact on people everywhere. Now, that is a life well lived.

Appendix A:
Ways to Increase Your Income

- **Art and design:** Artists can use websites such as Redbubble and CafePress to sell their designs on coffee mugs, T-shirts, or tote-bags. They can also use their artistic skills to create custom prints that can be sold directly or sold via downloaded file on sites such as Etsy.
- **Car washing/detailing:** People pay good money for on-site car washing and detailing services. Just coordinate a time with clients when they'll be home, bring your cleaning supplies, and use their water. Advertise by handing out business cards or flyers at local residences and businesses.
- **Consulting:** Consulting businesses can be started for a number of different purposes. If you're good at search engine optimization, you can start an SEO consulting company. If you're good at sales, consult about that. People also hire consultants for things such as organization, life coaching, career coaching, and a number of other reasons.
- **Errand running:** Many families today have two working parents who spend many hours a day working or carting kids around. They'll pay well for someone to grocery shop or run other errands for them.

- **Freelance writing:** If you have a talent for writing, there are many companies willing to pay well for your services. Check online sites such as Upwork for writing opportunities.
- **Handyman services:** If you know how to fix, repair, and improve things around the house, start a handyman business. Many people don't have the time or the know-how to care for or repair things around the house and will gladly pay for someone else to do it.
- **House cleaning:** If cleaning is your thing, you can start a house or office cleaning business. The services you offer can range from simple to extensive, depending on what you want to do. You can offer basic dusting, vacuuming, and cleaning services, or you can offer more extensive services such as carpet cleaning, drapery cleaning, window cleaning, etc. Market to local residents, businesses, and real estate rental companies.
- **House painting:** If you like indoor or outdoor painting, a painting service might be the way to go. Homeowners, business owners, and smaller towns often need people for both small and large painting jobs. Note that many states require professional house painters to obtain a license.
- **IT help:** Those who know how to set up or repair computers and/or websites can advertise their services at local coffeehouses, stores and restaurants, or online through sites such as Craigslist.
- **Landscaping:** If you like lawn work and working outdoors, consider starting a landscaping business. Your business can offer basic services such as mowing lawns and shoveling snow, or you can offer more comprehensive services such as design and landscape for yards.
- **Online affiliate marketing:** Thousands of companies such as Amazon, Republic Wireless, Personal Capital, and more will pay people well for selling their products. Start a blog or website where

you can market items to a specific audience and match client needs with the appropriate company.

- **Online courses:** Offering online courses in your area of expertise can produce a good income. You can offer your course through a video series or a series of scheduled emails.
- **Organization/decluttering:** If you've got a knack for organization, consider starting a business to help others get a handle on clutter and organize their homes. This is an area where many people want to be better but just don't know where to start.
- **Pet or child sitting:** If you enjoy children or animals, you can start a babysitting business, a pet sitting business, a dog walking business, a yard cleanup business for pet owners, or a dog training business.
- **Selling homemade items:** If you have a talent for knitting, sewing, woodworking, clothing design, or any other type of similar skill, you can create items to sell on sites such as Etsy or eBay.
- **Tutoring:** If you work well with children or college students and are smart in certain subjects such as math, science, or English, you can start a tutoring service. Get a step up on local tutoring centers by offering to come to the client's home and charging a lower price than local tutoring centers.
- **Writing ebooks:** Authors today write and sell ebooks on any number of subjects and sell them online with very little cash output. There are many, many resources online that will teach you how to write, publish, and sell your own ebook.

All of the previous business ideas require a minimal amount of cash output (usually under $5,000) so that you can start and run the business with cash, and there are many more ideas you can use to start a business with cash. Don't fall for the lie that you have to go into debt to start a business.

Appendix B: Glossary

The following terms will be helpful in learning about the stock market and planning your investment in it.

Asset allocation
"Asset allocation" refers to the practice of holding different types of assets (stocks, bonds, and real estate, for example) in your investment portfolio to help balance risk.

Balance sheet
A balance sheet is a financial statement detailing the financial position of a company on a specific date.

Bear market
Bear markets occur when consumer confidence is waning and stock prices are falling.

Broker
An individual (or company) who buys and sells investments for other people (for example, a stockbroker buys and sells stocks for customers).

Bull market
Bull markets occur when consumers are confident in the economy and stock prices increase.

Capital gain or loss
A capital gain is the profit that is made after sale of capital assets such as real estate, stocks, or bonds. A capital loss is a loss that is incurred after the sale of a capital asset.

Diversification

Diversification is the act of spreading your investment portfolio over and among a variety of different types of investment vehicles in order to minimize risk.

Expense ratio

The expense ratio of a mutual fund or exchange-traded fund is the amount you'll be charged annually to maintain the fund. In other words, if a fund has a 1 percent expense ratio, 1 percent of the fund's value will be used each year for administrative and other costs pertaining to the fund.

P/E ratio

The price-to-earnings ratio is the ratio of a company's current stock price to the company's reported earnings per share (the amount of total corporate earnings allocated to each share of outstanding stock).

Prospectus

A prospectus is a formal legal document that offers specific and pertinent information about an investment offered for sale to the public. A prospectus shares details such as a fund's objectives, investment strategies, expense ratios, and performance history, as well as information about a fund's management team.

Target-date fund

A target-date fund is an age-based mutual fund designed to hold an increasingly conservative asset allocation to minimize risk as the investor's target date approaches.

Yield

Yield pertains to the return on an investment.

Appendix C: Types of Businesses

There are many different types of businesses that can help you fund your ERP. Here are case studies for four different business ideas and how they can produce income to sustain early retirement.

Franchise-Based

Jameson bought into a franchise vending machine business that offered healthy snacks to customers. The start-up fee was $20,000, for which he paid cash, and it included a territory, two vending machines, supplies to get started with, and training for running and marketing the business successfully.

Jameson started promoting installation of his vending machines as soon as he finished training by marketing to sports studios such as dance, gymnastics, and self-defense studios. The studios liked that his machines offered healthy snacks instead of junk food, and so did parents whose children attended the classes.

Because he offered healthy, delicious snacks and placed his machines in exercise studios that did a lot of business, his average net income (after paying taxes and expenses) was $60 per month per machine. After a few years of growing his business, he had accumulated fifty vending machines and placed them throughout the large metropolitan area where he lived. At this point he was able to increase his income to about $3,000 per month after expenses.

Brick-and-Mortar Business

Michael and Erin decided to buy a local laundromat business to help fund their ERP. They bought an existing laundromat in an urban area in Arizona for $125,000. When they bought the business it was making a little over $30,000 per year. They made improvements to the laundromat in order to attract more customers. By doing some basic remodeling, keeping the facility clean, adding a small, inexpensive children's play area, installing two TVs, and offering free coffee, Michael and Erin made the laundromat a more pleasant place to be. Customers liked coming there because they hired friendly, helpful staff.

By the end of the second year, their net income from the laundromat had grown to $50,000 a year. By the end of the fifth year net income had grown to $90,000 per year, which was more than what they needed to fund their ERP. Since they'd used much of the income in those first five years to replace machines with energy-efficient models and build a substantial savings account for their business, profit is now high enough to fund their monthly ERP goal of $5,000 per month in income.

Online Income: Product Based

Justin wanted to start an online business using affiliate relationships to earn income. He started a blog that helped teach others how to get out of debt and build wealth. Justin wrote blog articles three times a week that taught people how to manage money. He also created a video course that taught basic financial principles. The site also offered affiliate links to products that would help readers manage their money well, such as links to sites that offered online budgeting help, books on personal finance, and links to reputable investing companies.

Justin worked hard at marketing the site by offering free guest posts to popular blog owners and by finding other ways to connect with the personal finance community. Within five years Justin's affiliate income was consistently over $10,000 a month. He received over 150,000 page views per month and did a great job of targeting his ideal audience through Facebook ads. His expenses consisted of paying the staff he hired to write articles for the site and help manage and promote social media channels—adding up to roughly $2,500 a month. His net income from the blog—which he now puts very little time into, is more than $7,000 per month.

Online Income: Service Based

Maya had a degree in graphic design, so she decided to open an online business that designs logos and T-shirts for businesses and blog owners. Maya is good at what she does. She has a gift for creating logos and T-shirt designs that draw in customers and are appealing to the eye. She started her business by contacting blog owners and business owners whose website logos could be more appealing, and by contacting online businesses that might profit from selling T-shirts.

At first, in order to attract clients, she charged only $100 for her logo design services and the same price for T-shirt designs. She was able to charge a lower fee because her overhead was low. The first couple of years weren't easy. Maya had to work hard to get her name out there and recruit clients. For the first year and a half, she had to continue working her full-time day job and also spend thirty hours a week trying to build her business. Once clients saw her work and how it improved their business, they were willing to give her references. Because part of her contract states that her design company information must be listed at the bottom of each website, her business grew. After two years she was able to raise her prices to $500 per logo design and $350 for T-shirt designs. Eventually, Maya hired other quality graphic designers to work on her team. She taught them to use the techniques that helped her make her business successful. She pays them one-fourth of each charged fee and keeps the remaining 75 percent for herself. Her business is now consistently designing at least twenty logos per month and five T-shirt designs per month, which gives Maya a gross income of $11,750 per month. After paying her employees twenty-five percent of that money, she nets approximately $8,812 per month at a minimum, which means Maya can meet her target ERP income of $3,750 a month after she sets aside $5,000 for taxes and other business expenses.

Appendix D: Resources

Book Recommendations

- *The Millionaire Next Door* by Thomas Stanley (Longstreet Press, 1996).

- *The Total Money Makeover* by Dave Ramsey (Thomas Nelson, 2013).

- *The Legend of the Monk and the Merchant* by Terry Felber (Thomas Nelson, 2012).

- *Think and Grow Rich* by Napoleon Hill (Chartwell Books, 2015).

- *The Little Book of Common Sense Investing* by John Bogle (Wiley, 2007).

All these books have helped me and my wife get to the financial state that we're in today. I highly recommend you read them as you work to achieve financial freedom.

Blog Recommendations

Reading personal finance blogs as you work your ERP will also help you stay on track with your plan. Following are some of my favorite money blogs.

- My personal blog, *Well Kept Wallet* (WellKeptWallet.com)

- *Mr. Money Mustache* (MrMoneyMustache.com)

- *Budgets Are Sexy* (BudgetsAreSexy.com)

- *Root of Good* (RootofGood.com)

- *Go Curry Cracker* (GoCurryCracker.com)

Podcast Recommendations

Listening to podcasts is a great way to help stay motivated to reach your early retirement goals. Here are the five podcasts that I think will be valuable resources to help you stay motivated.

- *Entrepreneur on Fire*

- *Well Kept Wallet*

- *Smart Passive Income*

- *Stacking Benjamins*

- *Money Peach*

Index

About the Author

Deacon Hayes is a financial expert, speaker, and podcaster. He is the founder of Well Kept Wallet, a financial education company that provides personal finance curricula for people across the world. He has been featured in many news outlets including *Yahoo! Finance, US News & World Report, Investopedia, CNNMoney,* and *Clark Howard.* He has helped thousands of people develop a financial game plan so that they can achieve their financial goals in life. Before starting his own company, he was a financial planner for an investment advisory firm assisting high net worth individuals. His passion is helping average people get from where they are to where they want to be with their career, money, and lifestyle.